CRACKS IN THE CRESCENT

An Appraisal of Pakistan's Enduring Fault Lines

CRACKS IN THE CRESCENT

An Appraisal of Pakistan's Enduring Fault Lines

Col Suraj Chambial, SM

Foreword by

Major General BK Sharma, AVSM, SM** (Retd.)

Director General, USI

Estd 1870

United Service Institution of India
New Delhi

PENTAGON PRESS LLP

First published in 2026 by
PENTAGON PRESS LLP
206, Peacock Lane, Shahpur Jat
New Delhi-110049, India
Contact: 011-26490600

Typeset in AGaramond, 11.5 Point
Printed at
Quiinkit Infotech Pvt. Ltd., Gurugram

ISBN 978-81-997728-8-5

Disclaimer: The views expressed in this book are those of the author and do not necessarily reflect those of the United Service Institution of India, New Delhi, or the Government of India.

www.pentagonpress.in

Contents

Foreword

Few nations in the modern world pose as complex, layered, and continuously evolving a challenge to India as Pakistan. Born in the crucible of Partition, Pakistan's national identity has long been shaped not only by what it stands for, but also by what it seeks to oppose. For more than seven decades, this fraught and often adversarial relationship has profoundly influenced regional security dynamics, strategic choices, and national psyches on both sides of the border.

Since 1947, Pakistan's journey has been marked by paradoxes – hope intertwined with disillusionment, ambition tempered by conflict, and moments of unity overshadowed by deep structural fissures. At the core of Pakistan's contemporary predicament lie enduring fault lines – ideological, ethnic, sectarian, economic, and geopolitical. These are not superficial cracks but deep chasms that define the very character of the state. From the persistent civil–military imbalance and the contested role of Islam in political life, to chronic ethnic discontent in Balochistan and Khyber Pakhtunkhwa, and enduring tensions with neighbours, each fault line has its own history, context, and strategic consequences.

Cracks in the Crescent: An Appraisal of Pakistan's Enduring Fault Lines, authored by Col Suraj Chambial, SM, offers a compelling and incisive examination of these structural vulnerabilities through a perspective grounded in India's strategic vantage point. The book unravels the complex threads of Pakistan's past and present, while offering a sober assessment of its possible future.

Pakistan stands at a critical crossroads today. Internally, it is struggling with a fragile economy, increasingly confrontational civil–military relations, rising extremism, demographic pressures, and acute climate vulnerabilities. The erosion of institutional legitimacy, coupled with growing provincial alienation, signals the possibility of multiple trajectories: economic collapse, political fragmentation, or yet another military-led reset. Externally, Pakistan's traditional strategic leverage is diminishing. Its manoeuvring space is narrowing under the weight of shifting global alignments, declining patronage, and a spotlight on its continued reliance on non-state proxies.

In addition to analysing these fault lines, the book outlines three plausible scenarios for Pakistan's future – stable, functional, or fractured – each built on the potential manifestation of widening structural divides. The author's arguments in each scenario are thought-provoking, offering valuable insights into how military dominance, cloaked in periodic civilian legitimacy, may shape Pakistan's trajectory.

Equally important is the debate on India's strategic options in dealing with an increasingly unpredictable Pakistan. The conduct of Pakistan – and the calibrated response of the international community – after Operation SINDOOR offers a striking example of geopolitics at play. India's challenge is not merely to anticipate what Pakistan might become, but to define how best to respond to it.

India's strategy must rest on realism, restraint, and readiness. Engagement, where necessary, should be guided by hard national interests rather than sentiment or pressure. Deterrence – both conventional and sub-conventional – must remain credible. Intelligence, diplomatic, and strategic efforts must move from reactive postures to anticipatory shaping of outcomes. Above all, India must insulate its rise from Pakistan's internal turbulence, even as it leverages global and regional partnerships to expose and counter destabilising actions emanating from across the border.

India cannot afford to be constrained by Pakistan's volatility. Strategic patience, calibrated firmness, and a long-term vision centred on regional stability must guide New Delhi's posture. By mapping Pakistan's potential pathways and India's corresponding strategic calculus, this book makes a meaningful contribution to an informed, objective, and forward-looking national debate.

The stakes remain high. A misjudgment could trigger conflict; a missed opportunity could stall peace. But a clear, unsentimental understanding of the road ahead offers the best chance for South Asia to move – however cautiously – from confrontation toward a more stable coexistence.

New Delhi
Jul 2025

Major General BK Sharma, AVSM, SM (Retd.)**
Director General, USI

Preface

Pakistan is a country of *intrigue and interest* for many reasons. Envisioned as a homogeneous homeland for Muslims in Indian sub-continent, Pakistan has already witnessed an enduring fragmentation (with creation of Bangladesh) which raises question on the very idea of its creation. Christened as a territory of immense strategic significance, Pakistan had the potential of playing a major role in the regional dynamics as well amongst the comity of Islamic nations. Unfortunately, Pakistan has repeatedly floundered on successive opportunities, exposing its infirmity in pursuing a long-term progressive strategy. Today, Pakistan has morphed into a state of major concern which is not only fragile internally but also remains a threat to the overall security edifice in the region.

Pakistan's relationship with India has always been *antagonistic and complex.* Pakistan's belligerence is deep rooted in history with characteristics of perennial hostility. Obsession with Kashmir and indignity of Bangladesh's separation has had an enduring impact on Pakistan's behaviour with India. It is therefore important for India to keep a close watch on events unfolding in Pakistan and maintain an active strategy for accomplishing desired deterrence against any misadventure. Study of the nature of the state and the inherent fault lines thus becomes extremely pertinent while taking into account the volatile geo-political and geo-strategic environment as prevalent.

The genesis of Pakistan's fault lines lies in the flawed creation of the state to a large extent. Pakistan incorporates a *multitude of cultures and ethnicities* which are endemically incongruent irrespective of the common thread of religion. Imposition of religion as a binding factor therefore was principally flawed which manifested in breakaway of the Eastern Wing in 1971. Born with inherent insecurities, Pakistan lacked the basic constituents of a nation state. The polity which secured separation from India and independence from the British rule failed to amalgamate the distant voices from every section of the society. Resultantly, political void facilitated military to seize power, portraying themselves as the saviour of the nation. Military dictators have repeatedly usurped power with impunity, becoming resentfully stronger and more assertive.

Pakistan's relationship with Afghanistan has also emerged as a major Faultline in Pakistan. The great game in the region has done greater harm to Pakistan than any good, resulting in a situation which is becoming increasingly difficult to untangle. Pakistan's relation with the west has traversed through *periods of tacit bonhomie to convoluted tragedies.* Pakistan's romance with so called Mujahideens or terrorists has started turning sour with most of these organizations turning hostile. In the last two decades approximately 30,000 people (both security forces and civilians) have lost their lives in terrorist attacks. Rising casualties has significantly dented the image of Pakistan Army, putting them on a backfoot. Pakistan is gradually getting sucked into the vicious cycle of violence which would be extremely difficult to contain.

Pakistan's iron bond with *big brother China* has also suffered periodic stress and strain amidst increasing security threats to China's assets and investments in the country. Pakistan's erratic economy is caught in a downward spiral once again desperately surviving on IMF bailouts and frequent doles from friendly countries. Irrespective of all of the above and multiple catastrophes, Pakistan has managed to stay afloat and remains a country which *'Fails to Fail'*. It is in this context and overall relevance of Pakistan to India that relevant fault lines merit due analysis to ascertain future trajectory of Pakistan and formulate India's strategic engagement with its western neighbour.

The book attempts to identify the future scenarios for Pakistan as a consequence of various fault lines. As a takeaway, a *framework of strategic toolkit* for India has been suggested which is important not only to maintain ascendancy over Pakistan but also to ensure unhindered growth of India as a regional and global power by 2047.

Acknowledgements

At the outset, I must admit that the journey for a *'Doc Marten'* soldier to imbibe geo-strategic wisdom as a *'scholar-warrior'*, has been equally exhilarating as it has been challenging. As I bring this research endeavour to a close, it is no less than a surprise for me that the efforts of last one year has finally taken the shape of this book titled as *"Cracks in the Crescent: An Appraisal of Pakistan's Enduring Fault Lines"*.

First and foremost, I extend my deepest gratitude to United Service Institution of India (USI), New Delhi for providing me the opportunity to undertake the research. I am thankful to *Major General Rajender Singh Yadav, VSM (Retd)*, Director CS3, USI and *Major General BK Sharma, PVSM, SM** (Retd)* Director General USI for providing unflinching support and guidance throughout the course of my academic pursuit.

I would not have realized this dream without the mentorship and patient handholding of my guide, *Major General Girish Kalia, VSM, AVSM.* He not only steered me through the complex rigors of scholarship but also shared his in-depth perspective on the subject which helped me in adding real value to the compilation. I must state that the fruit of this labour is as much a testament of my guide's vision as it is to my own effort.

I also acknowledge the invaluable contribution of scholars, subject matter experts and researchers who have shared their perspectives and insights on the subject. Writings of prominent scholars on Pakistan to include Christophe Jaffrelot, Stephen Philip Cohen, Tilak Devasher, Ayesha Siddiqa, Hussain Haqqani and many more has significantly helped me in shaping the research and understanding the complexities of Pakistan. Their literary work which I have cited extensively has not only enriched the quality of research but has also added the much-needed shine to the final product. I would fail in my duty if I don't mention the seminal work on the subject undertaken by *Brigadier*

Tapas Kumar Misra, YSM, VSM, which provided me the foundation for building up my research work.

Special thanks are also due to my peers and colleagues for innumerable sessions of constructive discussions as also to my family and friends for their patience and encouragement during the course of this work. I am once again grateful to USI for giving me this opportunity to conduct the study. Any errors or oversights that remain are entirely my own responsibility.

New Delhi
Jul 2025

Col Suraj Chambial, SM
Senior Research Fellow, USI

Abbreviations

BLA	Baluchistan Liberation Army
BRI	Belt and Road Initiative
CPEC	China-Pakistan Economic Corridor
DIME	Diplomatic Informational Military Economic
FATA	Federally Administered Tribal Areas
FATF	Financial Action Task Force
FCR	Frontier Crimes Regulation
FDI	Foreign Direct Investment
GWOT	Global War on Terrorism
ICG	International Crisis Group
ISI	Inter-Services Intelligence
ISIS-K	Islamic State of Iraq & Syria – Khorasan Province
ISPR	Inter Services Public Relations
IWT	Indus Waters Treaty
JeM	Jaish-e-Muhammed
JuD	Jamaat-ud-Dawa
JUI	Jamaat Ulema-e-Islam
KP	Khyber Pakhtunkhwa
LeJ	Lashkar-e-Jhangvi
LeT	Lashkar-e-Tayyeba
NFU	No First Use
NPT	Nuclear Non-Proliferation Treaty

NSG	Nuclear Suppliers Group
NWFP	North West Frontier Province
OIC	Organization of Islamic Cooperation
PTI	Pakistan Tehreek-e-Insaf
PTM	Pashtun Tahafuz Movement
SCO	Shanghai Cooperation Organization
SSP	Sipah-e-Sahaba Pakistan
TNW	Tactical Nuclear Weapons
TTP	Tehrik-e-Taliban Pakistan
WHO	World Health Organization
WTO	World Trade Organization

Chapter One

Pakistan: A Deceitful Birth

"There may be arguable grounds for maintaining that Muslims in India are a separate nation. But I have never heard it said that there are as many nations as there are religions on earth."

—**Mahatma Gandhi**[1]

Creation of a country is not an ordinary event and Pakistan was no exception. The complexity of Pakistan is largely derived from the situation that existed during the British rule in India and what transpired consequently eventually leading to partition. While all parties had galvanized to ensure ouster of British from India, there were also simultaneous voices amongst prominent political factions echoing internal dissent and disagreement. Demand for Pakistan was also one of the manifestations of this dissent. The idea of a separate state for Muslims of Indian subcontinent was not very obsolete. Most lucid exposition of the inner feelings of Muslim community was given by Muhammad Iqbal in his Presidential address at the All India Muslim League Session at Allahabad in 1930.[2] He suggested that for the healthy development of Islam in South-Asia, it was essential to have a separate identity for Muslim of the region. Three years after his Allahabad address, a group of Muslim students at Cambridge, headed by Chaudhry Rehmat Ali, issued a pamphlet, *'Now or Never'*, in which name of the proposed state for Muslims was christened as 'Pakistan' drawing letters from the Muslim majority regions of India.[3] The movement finally yielded result in 1947 with the creation of Pakistan. Today, the compulsions, convictions and circumstances that exited at the time of the birth of Pakistan still continue to influence her behaviour. It is therefore mandatory that an honest review of those conditions are carried out before discussing the characteristics of the Pakistani state whose fate has been permanently attached with that of India in the subcontinent.[4]

Advent of Muslims in India

For millennia, ideas, people and goods had moved freely between the Indian subcontinent and what is now the Middle East, with routine trade well established by 6th century CE. Even in the pre-Islamic era, Arab traders used to visit the Malabar region which linked them with the ports of South East Asia. According to historians Elliot and Dawson, the first ship bearing Muslim travellers was seen on the Indian coast as early as 630 AD.[5] The Indian rulers welcomed these traders and provided them with all facilities including landed property and freedom of religion leading to greater growth of Muslim influence. In 660 CE the second caliph, Umar, sent the first Arab expedition to Sindh and in 712 CE the province was conquered by Mohammad Bin Qasim. Along with advanced military power came missionaries and traders and the process of conversion to Islam began. Though the Arabs captured considerable territory, they were not able to retain power due to lack of knowledge about the art of administration and government. This conquest did not last long and with the death of Muhammad Bin Qasim the first chapter of Muslim occupation came to an end. Arab conquest of Sindh was a significant event which left a deep impact of Muslim culture in the Indian subcontinent.

Though the Muslims launched a number of invasions against India, they never thought of establishing their rule in the sub-continent till the twelfth century. Shahabudin Ghori (1175–1206 CE) was the first to instate an occupational empire annexing Multan, Sindh and Lahore.[6] He subsequently annexed Ajmer, Kanauj, Banaras and beyond. His successors extended the empire to Gwalior, Kalinjar, Gujarat, Bengal and Bihar. Thus within thirty years the entire region between Indus and Brahmaputra parsed into the hands of the Muslims laying firm foundation of Muslim rule in India. After the Ghoris, Khiljis, Tughlaq, Sayyid and Lodhi dynasties brought more territory under Muslim control. One very peculiar feature of the Muslim rule in India was that unlike the former invaders who came to adopt the Indian culture including language, manners, religion, dress and ideas within few generations of their settlement in India, the Mohammedans retained their independent entity failing to reconcile with the polytheistic belief system of indigenous Indians. Naturally, the members of two communities lived in the same land, retaining respective religious identities while unconsciously fusing at the cultural and societal level. The British formally disbanded the empire in 1858, at which time about one-quarter of India's population were Muslims. They were concentrated in East Bengal, the Northwest Frontier, Punjab, Sindh and Baluchistan, with large Muslim minorities in present-day Uttar Pradesh and Madhya Pradesh.

Because of wide regional variations, the impact of Islam on India is difficult to summarize. In the South and the East, Muslim rule was relatively benign and inclusive. In Hyderabad-Deccan and Bengal, Muslim rulers presided over vast Hindu populations and conversion was extensive and peaceful. In some instances, Hindu institutions received state patronage and there were extensive inter-religion marriages between Muslim ruling families and their high-caste Hindu counterparts, as family ties were used to shore up political alliances. Gradually, many Muslim dynasties, especially the Mughals, became more 'Indianized' through marriages and communions between Muslim and Hindu princely states. Thus, cultural evolution spanning over a period of more than five centuries, lead to distinct metamorphosis of Indian society divided across Muslim and Indic faiths yet united in political identity.

Seeds of Partition

Partition was neither a consequence of irrevocable differences between the Hindu and Muslim population in India nor a political adventure of British while they hurriedly departed India. It was rather an outcome of several complex factors which unfolded in a period of extreme flux. This was a period of growing desperation for British to leave while India stood determined to break out of the shackles of British occupation. While independence movement gained traction in the 1930s, the disgruntlement amongst prominent Muslim voices also increased. Important events and factors that contributed towards cementing the demand for a separate state for the Muslims are elaborated below:

- **Divide and Rule Policy**. In 1857, the British were horrified to see Hindus and Muslims fighting side by side and under each other's command against the foreign oppressor. They vowed this would not happen again. "Divide et impera was an old Roman maxim, and it shall be ours", wrote Lord Elphinstone after the revolt of 1857. The policy of 'divide and rule' was used most productively by the British to maintain its imperial rule. They identified pre-existing ethno-religious division in the Indian society and then manipulated it to prevent unified challenge to its rule. The British gave preferential treatment to selected groups over others, which created distrust and resentment. Certain areas witnessed more development as compared to the rest exacerbating the divide in the society. The British also patronised higher education for specific communities and sections leading to a systematic class divide.[7] The policy of 'divide et impera' fomented separate consciousness among the two communities with overt British sponsorship. Muslim separatism and communal divide was a consequence of this strategy to a large extent.

- **Muslim League.** The period after the First War of Independence in 1857 was an era of socio-political churn in the history of undivided India. On the political front, this led to the founding of the Indian National Congress in 1885. While Congress remained the main force of resistance against British colonial rule, it fell out of favour with a large section of the Muslim population. The All India Muslim League was founded in 1906 out of the need for political representation of Muslims in the freedom movement. At first the league was encouraged by the British and was generally favourable to their rule, however the party soon aligned with the public aspirations and adopted self-government for India as its goal in 1913. For several decades the league and its leaders, notably Mohammed Ali Jinnah, called for Hindu-Muslim unity in a united and independent India, however, the sentiment gradually eroded with fractures appearing in the collective Muslim opinion. Alignment of Congress with Hindu organizations such as Arya Samaj and Hindu Mahasabha in the 1920s also widened the mistrust between Congress and Muslims.[8] By the time the British parliament enacted the Government of India Act, 1935, a sense of separation and alienation from Congress had already set in amongst larger section of Muslim population which was capitalized by the Muslim League. It was not until late 1930s that the league started professing a separate identity for Muslims in the overall political paradigm in British India.

- **Partition of Bengal, 1905.** British Raj reorganized the Bengal Presidency with partition of the province in 1905. The partition separated the largely Muslim majority eastern areas from predominantly Hindu dominated western region. Lord Curzon pronounced the partition in July 1905 which officially came into effect on October 16, 1905. The partition was met with widespread resistance. It not only impacted the Indian society but also influenced the political sentiments across all parties. The British justified the partition as an administrative necessity, however in reality it was a distinct strategy of divide and rule to weaken the nationalist movement. The partition not only fuelled communal tensions but also furthered antagonistic sentiment amongst the Hindu-Muslim population. The British government eventually reversed its decision in 1911 and reunited Bengal, however, the collective conscience of the society had been scarred permanently which manifested in destructive proportion at the time of partition.[9]
- **Separate Electorate.** Creation of Pakistan is also seen as a culmination of communal politics that started during the early decades of twentieth century. Separate electorates created for Muslims by the colonial government in 1909 and expanded in 1919, crucially shaped the nature of communal politics. Separate electorates meant that Muslims could now elect their own representatives in designated constituencies.[10] This created a temptation for politicians working within this system to use sectarian slogans and gather a following by distributing favours to their own religious groups. Religious identities thus acquired a functional use within a modern political system and the logic of electoral politics deepened and hardened these identities. Community identities no longer indicated simple difference in faith and belief but came to mean active opposition and hostility between communities. Communal identities were further consolidated by a host of other developments in the early twentieth century.
- **Nehru Report.** In 1928 All Party Conference in British India prepared a memorandum which came to be known as Nehru Report. It proposed a federal set-up of government and a new dominion status for India's

constitution. Surprisingly, the chair of the report was Motilal Nehru while Jawaharlal Nehru acted as the secretary. The report called out for major reforms in the constitution and outlined the idea to have joint electorates with reserved seats for minorities. The report proposed a federal system of government with legislative powers concentrated with the central government. This was worked out to get together the diverse regions of India under a single but decentralized federal structure. Nehru Report did not propose separate electorates for religious or ethnic minorities. Instead, it allowed reserving minority seats in proportion to the population to ensure fair representation. The Nehru Report is significant as it embodies India's initial attempt at drafting a constitution. Surprisingly, the Nehru Report triggered a vehement reaction form the Muslim League. Muslim League proposed their own demands which was called as Jinnah's 14 Pointers highlighting special allowances for the Muslims. According to Mohammad Ali Jinnah Nehru Report was partisan. It was rejected by the Muslim League as it failed to address their demand for separate electorates and by radical nationalists who wanted complete independence instead of dominion status.

- **Socio-economic Factors.** Various socio-economic factors in the 19th and 20th century contributed to economic and social dissent fuelling separatist agenda. In contrast to Muslims, the Hindus were well-positioned to capitalise on the business opportunities created by colonial trade and enthusiastically embraced Western education. Muslims were averse to modern education and struggled to engage effectively in the emerging modern economy, hindered by institutions unsuitable for establishing large, enduring enterprises capable of efficient resource reallocation. Muslims had lower literacy and inadequate representation in industry/commerce, leading to economic backwardness. Muslims also worried that their economic interests would not be safeguarded in a Hindu-majority India. Landed Muslim elites in Punjab/Bengal saw creation of a separate state for Muslims as an opportunity for greater economic dominance spurred by ambition for greater power. Debates over national language exacerbated differences.[11] Popularity of Hindi language further alienated many

Muslims who favoured Urdu. This linguistic divide worsened the communal tensions and paved the way for a consolidated demand for a separate identity.

- **Elections of 1937**. The provincial elections of 1937 marked a pivotal moment in the history of British India, as it set the stage for the formation of Congress Ministries. Taking place against the backdrop of a rapidly changing political landscape, this election played a crucial role in shaping the trajectory of India's struggle for independence. In these elections, only 10 to 12% of the population exercised their right to vote. The Indian National Congress emerged as a prominent political force during this period, garnering widespread support and securing significant victory. As a result, Congress leaders assumed control of several provincial governments, laying the groundwork for the establishment of Congress Ministries. This transformative phase not only reflected the evolving dynamics of Indian politics but also signalled a shift in the power dynamics between the colonial rulers and the nationalist movements that would eventually culminate in the broader quest for self-rule. The Congress did well in the elections, winning an absolute majority in five out of eleven provinces and forming governments in seven of them. It did badly in the constituencies reserved for Muslims, but the Muslim League also fared poorly, polling only 4.4% of the total Muslim vote cast. The League failed to win a single seat in the North West Frontier Province (NWFP). It could capture only two out of 84 reserved constituencies in Punjab and three out of 33 in Sind.[12] In the United Provinces, the Muslim League could not form an independent government. This rejection in the elections convinced the League that if India remained united, then Muslims would find it difficult to gain political power because they would remain a minority. The League assumed that only a Muslim party could represent Muslim interests and that the Congress was essentially a Hindu party. Jinnah's insistence that the League be recognised as the 'sole mouthpiece' of Muslims could convince few at the time. Though popular in the United Provinces, Bombay and Madras, social support for the League was still fairly weak in three of the provinces from which Pakistan was to be carved out just ten years later – Bengal, the NWFP and the Punjab. Even in Sind it failed to form a government. It was from this point onwards that the League doubled its efforts at expanding its social support to wield greater power.

- **Communal Antagonism in India.** Communalism saw a distinct escalation towards the later years of 19th century. Friction between primarily the Muslims and the ethnic faiths increased in the early 1920s and 1930s. Muslims got antagonized by factors like cow protection movement, Vidhya Mandir Scheme, imposition of Vande Mantram as national song and efforts of organizations like Arya Samaj to bring back converted Muslims back to the folds of Hindu religion. Similarly, Hindus were enraged by the aggressive activities of tabligh (propaganda) and tanzim (organisation) after 1923.[13] The middle-class strata from either of the religious blocks assertively mobilized respective populations to build greater solidarity which led to rampant riots and incidents of violence across various parts of the country. However, it would be incorrect to infer that creation of Pakistan was an outcome of communal friction alone. Overall, the major reasons for growth of communalism can be attributed to:
  - Socio-economic backwardness of Muslims.
  - The revivalist nature of Socio-cultural reform movements.
  - Propagation of Hindus and Muslims self-interests.
  - British Policy of 'Divide and Rule'.
  - Role of personalities like Iqbal and Jinnah who felt Muslims would be marginalized in a united India.
  - Focus of Muslim League after the defeat of the 1937 elections and emergence of Pakistan Resolution, 1940.
  - A landslide victory of the Muslim League in the elections of 1946.

By early 1940s the political as well as social atmosphere in British India was distinctly divided across communal contours with both Hindus and the Muslims aspiring for greater prominence. However, demand for a separate state for Muslims with the idea for Pakistan came much later worsened by inability of British Raj to uphold its authority in the post-World War II geo-political environment.

The Two Nation Theory

The two-nation theory was an ideology of religious separatism that advocated Muslim nationhood, with separate homelands for Indian Muslims and Indian Hindus within a decolonised British India, ultimately leading to the Partition in 1947. In order to grasp the nuances of two-nation theory it is important to examine the philosophical strands in Muslim political thought which supported this idea. Muhammad Ali Jinnah was a firm believer Muslims of South Asia constituted a separate 'nation' by virtue of a distinct cultural identity. This itself is debatable as religion alone cannot be the only attribute of culture. According to Jinnah, it was impossible for Hindus and Muslims to co-habit as one nation as their religions were so vastly different. Besides, he felt that in a united India, Muslims would remain a minority and their interests would be overlooked or undermined, curbing their prosperous growth. Hence in his opinion it was necessary that a separate sovereign identity must be crafted for the Muslims of the subcontinent. Interestingly though, when Pakistan was finally envisioned, Jinnah spelt out a framework of secular character of the state which reflects the dichotomy of conflicting ideas of Pakistan envisioned by the founding father of Pakistan.

In order to critically understand the two nation theory, it is important to examine the Presidential address of Jinnah to the Muslim League in Lahore in 1940. In his address, Jinnah upheld the primacy of Muslim League as the sole political voice of Muslims of the subcontinent. He argued that in Provinces where Congress gained majority after the 1937 elections, the interest of Muslims was ignored. He urged the Muslims to re-organize themselves as a separate political entity and break away from the fallacious influence of Congress which was incapable of representing them adequately. Jinnah also voiced his disagreement with Gandhi on the question of minorities' rights in independent India. He pointed out that Congress was dominated by Hindus and was ignoring Muslim concerns. He feared that the Constituent Assembly would also be dominated by Hindus and so would independent India, leaving no space for rightful representation of Muslims.

Jinnah believed that in Islam, religious and political beliefs are not separated from each other. The mosque not only constitutes a place of worship but also the Assembly Hall. Hence, Hindu-Muslim unity or nationalism, signifying homogeneity between them in all non-religious matters, is unimaginable. The

Islamic polity in which religion and politics are inseparably united requires perfect isolation for its development. The idea of a common state with heterogeneous membership is alien to Islam and can never be fruitful. He believed that if the British were concerned about peace in the region, they would need to support the creation of a separate homeland for Hindus and Muslims. This would be the only way of avoiding communal conflict as both communities would have room for political self-expression and there would remain no reason for antagonism. In brief this was the explanation that Jinnah offered for his two-nation theory. Clearly, according to this theorization not much was said about equality between upper and lower classes of Muslims rather an attempt was made to silently pave the way for consolidating the domination of upper class Muslims.

It is critical to note that even though Jinnah is seen as the founder of Pakistan, another important political figure whose thoughts added to the fructification of the two-nation theory was Muhammad Iqbal. Iqbal had for the first time put forward the idea of a separate Muslim state, constituting the Muslim majority provinces in the West and North West India at the historical meeting of All India Muslim League in 1930 at Allahabad. Iqbal emphasised upon the cultural aspect of Islam and suggested that Muslims should come together to create a geo-political identity. He suggested that each region in the world had its own specific addition to Islam and in order to ensure that Muslims of that region flourish, they must come together both socially and politically. Islam was the basis of identity and this must translate into political identity as well. The concept of territorial nationalism was critical to his thought. Nationalism as a concept was seen to be important only in so far as it served as a point of merger between Muslim identity and Islam. Iqbal found Indian nationalism problematic because it did not adequately recognize Muslim identity. He was sceptical of an independent India characterized by the domination of Hindus. The most interesting aspect of Iqbal's assertion of Muslim political identity was that he argued for provisional autonomy for Muslim dominated areas within an Indian Union.

It is important to point out that Muslim political thought was not homogeneous. There were currents in Muslim political thought which supported the two nation theory, as well as opposed the two nation theory. There existed a strand of Muslim nationalism in colonial India which believed in secularism. This ideology can be seen in the work of Abdul Kalam Azad. Azad believed in the idea of composite Indian nationalism. He believed, like Gandhi that Muslims and Hindus could peacefully co-exist and grow together, within a united nation state. Azad based his beliefs on the scriptural thesis of Quran. His main aim was the integration of the *millat* (a form of community) and adoption of principles of *shariat* by all Muslims. Azad supported the theorization of *'wahdat-e-adyan'* (unity of all religions).[14] He believed in the unity of all religions and the common purpose of all religions as the elevation of human spirit and inculcating faith in God. Respect was to be shown to all religions equally and there was no hierarchy amongst religions. For Azad the most important aspect of Islam was *'ruboobiyat'* (meaning mercy and justice) which he thought accrued to all humans irrespective of their religion or race. Azad did want to create space in Indian nationalism for a distinct Muslim identity but within a federative structure of power sharing.

The idea of a separate Muslim state was not supported by Muslim religious leaders as much as it was supported by certain struggling classes. These included the professional groups from Uttar Pradesh, Bihar, Hyderabad and the trading and banking communities of Gujarat, Bombay and Calcutta. These classes saw in the idea of Pakistan space for access to power for themselves and lesser competition. It also needs to be remembered that Pakistan was not the vision of all Muslims. It was the formulation of some politically powerful Muslims who had managed to secure bargaining power within their community and with the British. The Two-Nation Theory stands as a cornerstone of Pakistan's national identity and has played a pivotal role in shaping the country's history, politics, and societal fabric. Rooted in the belief that Hindus and Muslims in the Indian subcontinent are distinct nations with irreconcilable differences, this theory served as the ideological basis for the creation of Pakistan in 1947.

The Impact of World War II

Partition of India and creation of Pakistan also had its roots in the cataclysmic event of World War II. With Germany's invasion of Poland on 01 September, 1939 the Second World War broke out and on 03 September 1939, England declared war against Germany. Simultaneously India too was declared a belligerent when Viceroy Lord Linlithgow proclaimed over All India Radio from his summer residence in Shimla that the Government of His Majesty was engaged in war with Germany proclaiming a state of war emergency in British India as well. He pleaded to the people in British India and the Indian Princes to support the war effort. The war had brought with it deeper implications for the British imperialism. Britain had to negotiate terms with all the stakeholders in the Indian subcontinent in order to gain their support for the war. The urgent wartime requirement of Britain was to possess a mighty army and for this end the Indian soldiers had to be conflated into the British army. Britain was able to manoeuvre the Indian sentiments as around 2.5 million Indian army soldiers fought World War II under the flag of British Empire.[15] The mounting tension in Europe proved a blessing in disguise for the people of India, both Hindus and Muslims. Clouds of second World War gave an ideal opportunity to both National Congress and Muslim League to negotiate with the British seeking to obtain a more independent role in future of India.

The Second World War served as a catalyst for an unexpected shift in political power. Weakened by the war and facing mounting pressure from popular national movements – most notably the Congress under Gandhi's leadership – the British were compelled to reconsider their hold over India. In response to the Quit India Movement, London sent a mission headed by Sir Richard Stafford Cripps (the Cripps Mission) to New Delhi in early 1942. The British had assured the Congress that with their cooperation in the war effort the possibility of greater self-rule could be negotiated when the war ended. The Congress leaders, however, were not appeased. They insisted that Britain must allow for a transfer of power while the war raged which led to an impasse and failure of the mission. Contrarily, Jinnah-led Muslim League was less aggressive in seeking immediate British withdrawal. The differences between the two groups were not lost on Britain, who sensed an opportunity to capitalize it for their war effort.

Occupation of Iran, Iraq and Syria by the British Indian military evoked sharp criticism from the Muslim population. Resignation of Congress leaders from the ministries was also not appreciated. In order to appease the Muslims, both the Viceroy and the Secretary of State repeatedly gave assurance that no constitutional or administrative measure would be implemented without the consent of the League. British were trying to consolidate Muslim opposition to the Congress in order to secure support for their war effort. This consequently resulted in elevation of Jinnah's prestige and influence with the British. With Government's help the non-League ministries of Punjab, Bengal, Sind, Assam and North West Frontier Province were removed and brought under the rule of the League. Jinnah's strategy was to offer incentives to the British while threatening them with fearful consequences if they showed any inclination to accept demands of Congress especially against special privileges for the Muslims.

Second World War and growing consternation of the British with the Congress leaders cumulatively created a distinct space for Jinnah to build a strong relationship with the British. This also assisted him to strongly pitch for the demand of an independent Muslim state. Jinnah supported the British war effort, and bargained to argue that 'Islam was in danger'. By committing Muslim troops for the War effort, Jinnah secured frequent interactions with the Viceroy which he capitalized in garnering support for his plans and objectives. He prevailed upon the British, not to accept the demand put forward by the Congress leaders for a Constituent Assembly to frame the Constitution of India. He ensured that no constitutional arrangement is finalized which did not have the approval of Muslim League. Amidst the overall criticality of Second World War faced by the crown, one entity in Indian subcontinent that gained immensely was the Muslim League besides Jinnah individually who leveraged their position to elicit desired commitments and favours aligned to the philosophy of Muslim League.

The Second World War also played a role in further widening the divide between the Hindu and Muslim communities. Congress and Muslim League tried to exploit the Second World War to seek support for their respective demands. But both parties differed in their manner and tactics.[16] The Congress pressurized the Government through their policy of non-cooperation with withdrawal from the Provincial ministries while Muslim League capitalized the situation more shrewdly by adopting a policy of soft confrontation and smart negotiation. Jinnah ensured that the British commit to the cause of greater Muslim representation thereby consolidating the grounds for a separate Muslim state through shrewd political diplomacy.

Role Played by Mohammed Ali Jinnah

Mohammed Ali Jinnah was born on 25 December 1876 in Karachi, now in Pakistan, but then part of British India. His father was a prosperous merchant from a family of textile weavers belonging to a village named Paneli in the princely state of Gondal near Rajkot, Gujarat.[17] Jinnah had three brothers and three sisters, including his younger sister Fatima Jinnah. He started his education from an infant vernacular school while also attending a Gujarati medium Madrasa. From an early age he wanted to join the family business and despised going to school. However, his father always wanted him to pursue education for which he sent him to his aunt's place in Bombay. The exposure at Bombay had a profound impact on Jinnah. In the meanwhile, Jinnah's father was collaborating with Grahams Shipping and Trading Company, London which offered him an apprenticeship.[18] Soon after his arrival in London, Jinnah gave up the business apprenticeship and picked up law. The aspiring barrister joined Lincoln's Inn, where he was influenced by 19th century British liberalism, like many other future Indian independence leaders. He became an admirer of the likes of Dadabhai Naoroji and Sir Pheroze Shah Mehta. The Western world not only inspired Jinnah in his political life, but also greatly influenced his personal preferences.[19] In 1895, at an age 19 years, he became the youngest British Indian to be called to the bar in England.[20]

Upon his return to India, he joined Bombay High Court. Jinnah devoted much of his time to his law practice in the early 1900s but also remained politically involved. Jinnah joined Indian National Congress in 1906 and in those early years of his political career, he was a strong advocate of Hindu–Muslim unity and even helped to shape the 1916 Lucknow Pact between the Congress and the Muslim League. In December 1912, Jinnah addressed the annual meeting of the Muslim League although he was not yet a member. He joined Muslim League the following year, although he remained a member of the Congress as well and stressed that League membership took second priority to the 'greater national cause' of an independent India. In 1916, with Jinnah now president of the Muslim League, the two organisations signed the Lucknow Pact, setting quotas for Muslim and Hindu representation in the various provinces. In 1920, however, Jinnah resigned from the Congress when it agreed to follow a campaign of *satyagraha*, which he regarded as political anarchy.[21] In the subsequent years Jinnah drifted much farther away from Indian National

Congress and crafted his own political identity in Muslim League as a revered voice of Muslim interest in India.

Jinnah viewed that partition was necessary to safeguard the rights of Indian Muslims. Muhammad Ali Jinnah wrote an article published in the England 'Time and Tide' on 09 March 1940 saying that, "The British people being Christian sometime forget the religious wars of their own history and today consider religion as a private and personal matter between man and God. This can never be the case in Hinduism and Islam. Both these religions have definite social codes and aspect of their social life."[22] Again, addressing a historic public meeting at Lahore on 23 March, 1940 he said, "We have our past experience of the last two and half year. We have learnt many lessons. We are now apprehensive and can trust no body. It has always been taken for granted mistakenly that the Muslim are a minority. Muslims are a nation by any definition of a nation. Hindu and Muslims belong to two religions, philosophies, social customs and literatures. They neither inter-marry nor inter-dine and indeed belong to different civilizations which are based on conflicting ideas and conceptions. Their concepts of life are different. They have different epics, different heroes and different episodes. Very often the hero of one is the foe of the other and likewise their victories and defeat, overlap. Muslims are nation according to any definition of a nation and they must have their homeland, their territory and their state."[23]

Jinnah was a staunch believer of the Two Nation Theory and was convinced that the two communities could not co-exist together. Although, the idea of a separate political and sovereign Muslim identity germinated in the Aligarh school of thought, duly seconded by Iqbal. Citing the socio-economic condition of the Muslims Jinnah excelled in his communal propaganda. The defeat in 1937 elections was a wakeup call for the Muslim League after which their efforts to galvanize the community resulted in spread of greater communalism and demand for a separate Muslim state. Jinnah leveraged the fear and apprehension of Muslim population against a so-called Hindu domination to seek political mileage, which bore result in the form of political victory of Muslim League in the 1946 elections. Some scholars believe that the demand of Jinnah for a separate state was merely a bargaining chip with the Congress as he wanted a separate status for Muslims, but not a separate nation. However, this assumption is fraught with inconsistencies which are in conflict with other concurrent developments at that point in time. Muslim landlords (in Sindh and other areas of Pakistan) and elites who were against the model of socialist democracy propagated by Congress, were in favour of a separate nation. Jinnah vetoed every attempt by the Congress in talking with British officials to find an amicable solution. Jinnah and the Muslim League wanted to be the sole representatives of Muslims in India, and the demand for a separate state for an excellent aggregator.

Jinnah's orchestration of the 'Direct Action Day' on 16 August 1946 was symbolic of his individualistic aspirations for power and reflection of dwindling confidence of Muslim League leaders in Indian National Congress. 'Direct Action Day' was the day on which All India Muslim League gave a call for general strikes and economic shut down in support for its demand for a separate Muslim homeland after the British exit from India. Since Lahore Resolution of 1940, the Muslim League had been demanding constitution of 'independent states' for the Muslim-majority areas of India in the northwest and the east. In 1946, Cabinet Mission to India proposed a three-tier structure for transfer of power at the level of centre, groups of provinces and provinces which was rejected by Congress as well as Muslim League. On 16 July 1946, the Muslim League announced a general strike terming it Direct Action Day, to assert its demand for a separate homeland for Muslims in North Western and Eastern provinces of colonial India. The state of Bengal was one of those few pockets where Muslims were in majority. However, they were precariously positioned against a political hinterland inhabited by the Hindu dominated National Congress, the Communist Party of India and the Hindu Mahasabha.

While giving a call for Direct Action, Muhammad Ali Jinnah said that he saw only two possibilities 'either a divided India or a destroyed India'.[24] Against a backdrop of communal tension, the protest triggered massive riots in Calcutta in which more than 4,000 people died and 100,000 residents were left homeless within 72 hours. The violence sparked further religious riots in the surrounding regions of Noakhali, Bihar, United Provinces (modern day Uttar Pradesh), Punjab (including massacres in Rawalpindi) and the North Western Frontier Province. The events sowed the seeds for the eventual partition of India. Jinnah's call for the Direct Action Day was brutal and severed the belief that he was a liberal Muslim. The riots created a feeling of accentuated alienation amongst the Muslims, thereby further strengthening their desire for a separate nation.

The violence made both communities realise the extent of harm they were capable of causing to each other when being 'forced' to live together. The severity and the extent of the violence witnessed during the Calcutta killings gives testimony of the ideological divide that had been created between the two communities helmed by the insecurities and aspirations of Jinnah. 'Direct Action Day' in a way for the final nail in the coffin of a united India leading to eventual partition of British India and creation of Pakistan.

Birth of a Nation: Pakistan

The Muslims had constructed a theoretical paradigm to intellectually legitimize their demand of a separate homeland. The concept of 'Two Nation Theory' became a force to integrate and transform the energies of Muslims. The belligerent ethnic and communal divide in British India cannot be singularly censured for the eventual partition. The vitiated political environment accentuated by political insecurities of Jinnah and Nehru created conditions of irreconcilable differences leading to eventual breakdown of united front for independence from the British Raj. In other way the plurality of India (composition) eclipsed by inequality (environment) operating under imperialism (structure) left no other option than accepting the partition of India.

Apparently Muslim League and Congress had many similarities. Both the political parties were headed by lawyers and had Muslims in their ranks. They had the same agenda for several years to set India free from British colonial rule. They were together in Lucknow Pact (1916), Khalafat Movement (1919-1922), Swadeshi Movement and Civil Disobedience. However, gradually they emerged as two distinctive forces. Divisive policies of British and a western oriented political system culminated and further sharpened their dissimilarities. They were divided on common issues of political autonomy, self-rule, political representation and aspired model of democracy. The Congress believed in freedom of India from the British imperialism however, wanted to continue with British political system although this system had contrived communalism in India and caused dissatisfaction among the majority of non-Hindu Indians. Conversely, the Muslim League and Jinnah held the view that freedom is not only freedom from British but also freedom from the so called exploited majority of British India. As a consequence, all efforts to amalgamate the political voices against British rule to aspire for an undivided India failed miserably, which eventually lead to the birth of Pakistan.

The Indian Independence Act was passed on 18 July 1947 by the British Parliament to establish the independent dominions of India and Pakistan. It also ended the use of the title 'Emperor of India' for the British Crown and terminated all existing treaties with princely states. The act divided the territories into India and Pakistan based on the majority religion of the population. India was made up of all the territories under the King's sovereignty that were not designated as Pakistan. Pakistan was made up of East Bengal, Western Punjab, Sind, and Baluchistan. The North-West Frontier Province could join Pakistan if a referendum showed a majority in favour. Power was formally transferred to India and Pakistan on August 14, 1947. India gained its independence on August 15, 1947. Jawaharlal Nehru became India's first Prime Minister, and Muhammad Ali Jinnah became Pakistan's Governor-General. Liaquat Ali Khan became Pakistan's Prime Minister.

The partition of India led to the largest forced migration in history. Bengal in the East and Punjab in the West were too complex to be divided with ease. These provinces had a mixed population of Hindus and Muslims, without a clear majority of one of the two religious groups. The majority of India's Sikhs were also living in Punjab. In a period of only six weeks, the borders within these regions had to be decided. The British judge Cyril Radcliffe was appointed to lead the commissions that would determine the borders between India and Pakistan in Bengal and Punjab.[25] He did not have the time to visit the places where the borders were being drawn. As a result, he based his decision on an outdated census, comparing statistical proportions of Hindus, Muslims and Sikhs. The borders were finalized without taking into account the agrarian records, industry, basic infrastructure and social connections thereby cutting off communities from their roots. The borders were made public only on 17 August 1947, two days after the independence. Suddenly millions of people became a minority in their own community. Even though minorities were officially free to stay in their own country, many people decided to migrate. Some migrated because of ideological reasons, others because they feared for their lives. The Partition led to excessive ethnic violence. Groups of Hindus, Muslims and Sikhs attacked each other's villages and refugees. Neither of the two new countries had the power to maintain order. Estimates of the number of victims vary between roughly 200,000 to two million.[26] Approximately twelve to fifteen million people migrated and hundreds of thousands of women, often of a very young age, were abducted, abused and raped. Birth of Pakistan did bring initial jubilations to the Muslim community but the celebrations quickly dissipated due to horrors of communal violence that followed permanently scarring the conscience of both nations.

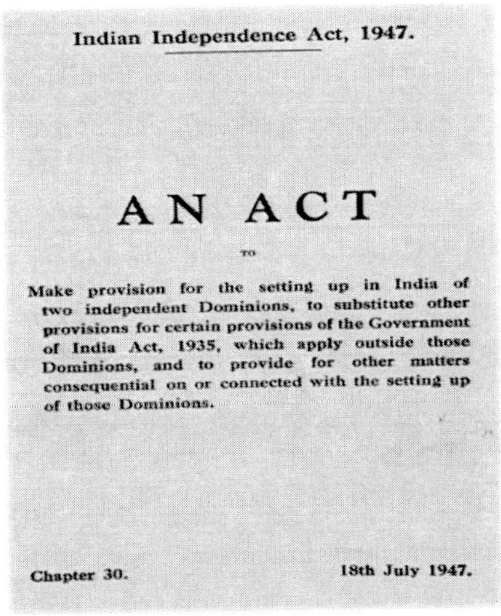

Indian Independence Act, 1947.

AN ACT

TO

Make provision for the setting up in India of two independent Dominions, to substitute other provisions for certain provisions of the Government of India Act, 1935, which apply outside those Dominions, and to provide for other matters consequential on or connected with the setting up of those Dominions.

Chapter 30. 18th July 1947.

Figure 1.1: Indian Independence Act, 1947

Pakistan: A Nation of Congenital Abnormalities

A detailed inquiry of relevant factors brings out that the creation of Pakistan to a large extent was not an event of natural process but a consequence of events and circumstances that became increasingly unsurmountable as the situation deteriorated during transition of power from British crown to the newly created states. As a result, Pakistan was born with distinct congenital inadequacies which remain relevant even today.

- **An Imperfect Idea of Pakistan.** Hindus and Muslims have lived together in the Indian subcontinent for several centuries. The relationship between the two prominent communities had transcended from tolerant coexistence to heightened belligerence. However, the Muslims population at large never aspired for a separate political identity till as late as early 1900s at the hands of British Raj which treated the divide between Hindus and Muslims as a policy advantage to meet their own ends.[27] The discontent amongst the Muslims against an apparent preferential treatment of the majoritarian Hindus by the British allegedly laid the foundation of Islamic Pakistan. Colonial policy sowed seeds of separatism among South Asian Muslims not only frustrated by systemic discrimination but also inspired from a flawed nostalgia of Mughal period. The dissolution of Mughal Empire meant losing a kingdom, language, culture, capital city, and sense of self amongst the Muslims of India. Prominence of Indian National Congress in the freedom struggle lead to gradual discontentment amongst the Muslim voices who wanted a larger say in the movement. Marginalization of Muslims by the British in the early 1900s was also a major driver for creating a separate political voice for Muslims of India. The idea of dividing India emerges from the political landscape that developed during the 1940s. Irrespective of the fact that the idea of Muslim Nationhood was not universally accepted, the politics of the day compounded by the disinterest of British in continuing in India created a situation which lend to division of India.

- **Flawed Federalism.** Muslim League secured partition of India and creation of a new Muslim state in 1947 which was accompanied by an unparalleled mass migration and loss of life. It is a fact that the amalgamated regions of Pakistan (both in the West and in the East) although with Muslim majority population had less in common with distinct divisions along social and cultural lines. These regions did not necessarily ascribe to the idea of Pakistan as conceived by Indian Muslim League. Whether it was Kalat, Sindh or the Agencies and Frontier Regions, abolition of British Raj did not translate into amalgamation into a unified state of Pakistan. The public opinion across all sections of the society was much fragmented with little acceptance for the idea of a nation state. Religion failed to bring together the pan Muslim population of Indian subcontinent when the British left which rightly manifested many years later with severing of East Pakistan and creation of Bangladesh. Such are the incongruencies in federal structures of Pakistan that even till date it is struggling with adoption of an idea of a perfect nation-state.

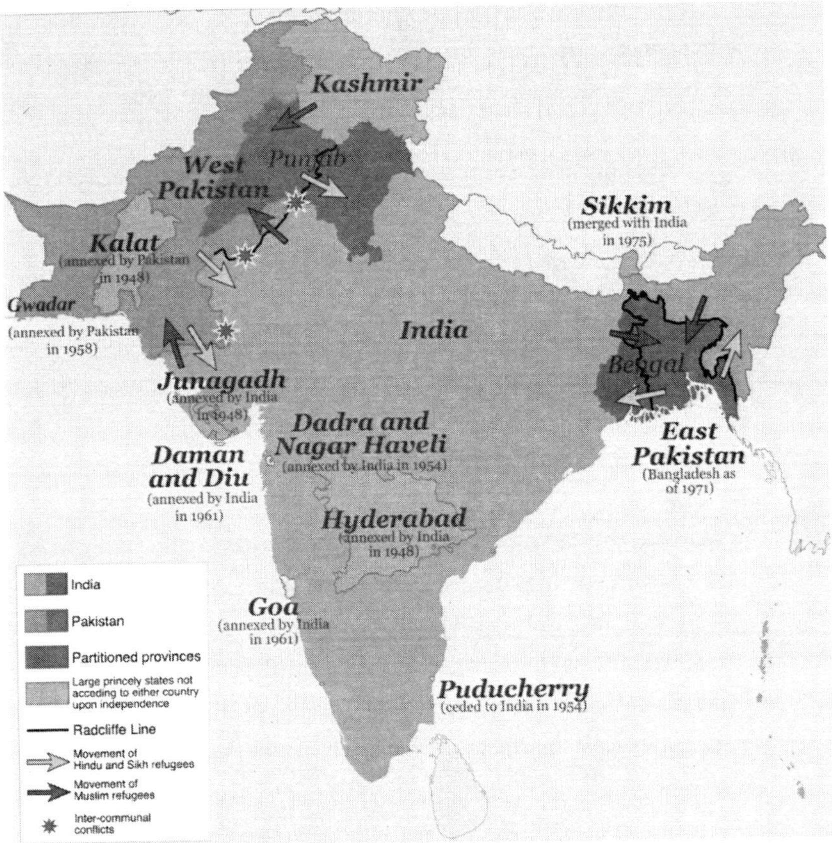

Figure 1.2: Partition Flashpoints

- **Political Fragility**. At partition, Pakistan lacked a real egalitarian political system for its diverse population. This subsequently led to chronic regional tensions and successive failure in forming a constitution as late as 1956.[28] Despite Jinnah's large claims, the Muslim League failed to build up effective party machinery in the Muslim majority provinces. The league had no real control over politicians or the populace that was mobilized in the name of Islam. Islam had certainly been a useful rallying cry, but it did not effectively translate into the solid support that Jinnah and the League needed post creation of Pakistan. The diversity of Pakistan's provinces was a potential threat to central authority. While the provinces continued to be the main centres of political activity, those who set about creating the centralized government in Karachi were either politicians with no real support or civil servants trained in the old traditions of British Indian administration. The inherent weaknesses of the Muslim League's structure, together with the absence of a central administrative apparatus that could coordinate the affairs of the state, proved to be a crippling disadvantage to Pakistan.

- **Islam: A Binder or Divider.** Since religion had played an important role in the creation of Pakistan, its role in the overall context of an independent Pakistan assumed major significance. Pakistan, was the only country established in the name of Islam, with overwhelming support from Muslims, especially in provinces like the United Provinces, where Muslims were a minority. Jinnah, closely associated with the ulama, was described upon his death by Maulana Shabbir Ahmad Usmani as the greatest Muslim after Aurangzeb, aspiring to unite Muslims under Islam.[29] However, the experiment with Islam soon proved counterproductive as it failed to unify the cross ethnic population across the new state and the political leadership as it had been expected. East Pakistan's Bengali Muslims outrightly opposed the idea of an Islamist state. There was dissonance regarding the role Islam should play in the social and political order of the country. The persistent disagreement on the subject diminished the power of Islam as the locus standi for affective identity. Feudalism and economic disparity further undermined the liberal political system which the elites wanted to establish. Jinnah, from the very inception of the state, made it clear that Pakistan was not going to be a theocratic state ruled by religious priests. Advocating equal citizenship to all communities and hinting at religious freedom which would unshackle any kind of religious identity, in his inaugural address to the Constituent Assembly, he said "...in the course of time, Hindus will cease to be Hindus, and Muslims will cease to be Muslims, not in the religious sense because that is the personal faith of the individual, but in the political sense as citizens of one nation."[30] The political elites of Pakistan, comprising the Muslim bourgeoisie, feudal lords and bureaucratic elites, were not in favour of an Islamic state, rather they wanted to confine the role of Islam to cultural identity. Religion was supposed to be the binding factor and raison d'etre for Pakistan, unfortunately identity of a nation state required much more.

- **Equal-Unequal Partition.** The plan to divide the Indian subcontinent into the successor states of India and Pakistan was officially announced on 3 June 1947. Creating India and Pakistan as two sovereign nation-states involved a division of governmental staff, properties, records of civil departments, armed forces, financial settlements, marking out the separate jurisdiction of the high courts and federal courts, charting out domicile policies and of course, demarcation of boundaries. To administer the endless nitty-gritty of the transfer process, 10 expert committees were formed, consisting of high-ranked bureaucrats. These committees had an equal number of Muslim and non-Muslim officers representing the interests of two future governments. The real work of partition – the division of assets and liabilities – began in an atmosphere marked by a heightened sense of religious nationalism and aggressive communal sentiments. The entire process of partition was determined by these two opposing sentiments – that of suspicion, on one hand, and cooperation, on the other. Delhi was already the capital of undivided India and a system was in place. Similarly, Calcutta too had the necessary set-up. However, the scene was very different in Karachi or in Dhaka. One of the biggest issues before the Partition Council was the division of the defence forces. Under this exercise, two-thirds of the force remained in India while one-third were sent to Pakistan. Another big challenge for India was the division of the money between the two countries. According to the Partition agreement, Pakistan received 17.5 per cent of the assets and liabilities of British India. In addition to the financial and military assets, India and Pakistan also reached a consensus on the division of other movable assets. All moveable assets were divided in the ratio of 80:20. Irrespective of the attempted fairness in partition of the assets, India was much stable in tackling the issues of a new nation while Pakistan was left with challenges that were disruptive and relatively more challenging.

Creation of Pakistan on departure of British Raj was a greater consequence of political disagreement rather than a considered thought to create a separate nation state. To an extent, the credit for germinating the idea of irreconcilable co-existence between the Hindus and Muslims also goes to the British who patronised the 'Two Nation Theory' premised on a preferred Divide and Rule policy. Culturally and socially, both Hindu and Muslim communities had greater tolerance for each other at the grassroots level that what was made out of it by the political leadership of Indian Muslim League. However, once the seeds of discontent were sown amongst the Muslims that they would not be able to retain their identity as a larger minority in India, the idea of separate nation started getting more traction. In the beginning, it was an idea which held great attraction for the larger masses mounted on the pedestal of religion and assumed power that it generates. However, the flawed construct of an independent nation state premised on a religious thread soon lost its lustre and greater problems started to beckon Pakistan. The inherent faults at multiple levels developed during the birth of Pakistan weakened the state which continues to challenge Pakistan even today. Religion, situations, leaders and subsequent course taken by Pakistan through several decades after 1947 has rendered Pakistan not only more vulnerable but extremely fragile, transforming into a major security concern in the region.

Notes

1 M.K. Gandhi, "*The Collected Works of Mahatma Gandhi*", Vol. 74. New Delhi: Publications Division, Ministry of Information and Broadcasting, Government of India, 1979.

2 Sevea, I.S. (2012), "*The Political philosophy of Muhammad Iqbal: Islam and Nationalism in Late Colonial India*". https://ci.nii.ac.jp/ncid

3 Chaudhry Rehmat Ali, (1933), "Now or Never: Are We to Live or Perish Forever?", Cambridge: Self-published.

4 Embassy of Islamic Republic of Pakistan, "*History of Pakistan*", https://www.pakistanembassytokyo.com.

5 Henry Miers Elliot, John Dawson, (2013), "*The History of India as told by its own Historians*", Cambridge University Press.

6 Richard Eaton, (2019), "*India in the Persianate Age: 1000-1765*", Penguin Books Ltd.

7 "*Education in British India*", https://oxfordre.com.

8 "*The Khaksar movement and Muslim mobilization in the 1930s India*", Times of India, 27 Apr 2023.

9 Vinod Kumar Saxena, "*The Partition of Bengal (1905-1911)*", Kanishka Publishing House.

10 MN Das, (2017), "*India under Morley and Minto: Politics behind Revolution, Repression and Reforms*", Routledge Library Editions.

11 BR Ambedkar, *"Pakistan or Partition of India' (1945)"*, Create Space Independent Publishing Platform.

12 "*Understanding Partition*"; https://ncert.nic.in.

13 *ibid.*

14 Sammena Kausar, *"Literature, Theology, and Abdul Kalam Azad"*, https://contendingmodernities.nd.edu.

15 Annu Palakunnathu Matthew, "*The Unremembered- Indian Soldiers of World War-II*", https://quod.lib.umich.edu.

16 "*Indian National Movement*", https://www.iipa.org.in.

17 Ayesha Jalal, (1985), "*The Sole Spokesman: Jinnah, the Muslim League, and the Demand for Pakistan*", Cambridge University Press.

18 Stanley Wolpert, (1984), *"Jinnah of Pakistan"*, Oxford University Press.

19 ' *Muhammed Ali Jinnah – Biography*', https://www.britannica.com.

20 Husain and Mahmud, *"Mohammed Ali Jinnah | Biography, Accomplishments, Religion, Significance, & Facts,"* Encyclopaedia Britannica, July 20, 1998, https://www.britannica.com/biography/Mohammed-Ali-Jinnah.

21 Stanley Wolpert (1984), *'Jinnah of Pakistan'*, Oxford University Press.

22 Muhammad Ali Jinnah, *"The Constitutional Future of India,"* Time and Tide (London), March 9, 1940.

23 Stanley Wolpert (1984), *'Jinnah of Pakistan'*, Oxford University Press.

24 *'Remembering Direct Action Day'*, https://www.telegraphindia.com,.

25 Yasmin Khan, (2007), *"The Great Partition: The Making of India and Pakistan"*, Yale University Press.

26 Urvashi Butalia, (1998), *"The Other Side of Silence: Voices from the Partition of India"*, Viking Penguin.

27 Ayesha Jalal, (2000), *"Self and Sovereignty: Individual and Community in South Asian Islam since 1850"*, Routledge.

28 Ian Talbot, (2005), *"Pakistan: A Modern History"*, Hurst & Company, London.

29 Venkat Dhulipala, (2015), *"Creating a New Medina: State Power, Islam, and the Quest for Pakistan in Late Colonial North India"*, Cambridge University Press, New Delhi.

30 Ziad Haider, *'Islam and the Early History of Pakistan'*, https://www.hoover.org

Chapter Two

Geo-Strategic Importance of Pakistan

"Pakistan is too nuclear to fail, too Islamist to ignore and too dysfunctional to fully trust."

—Stephen Cohen[1]

Pakistan holds immense geopolitical significance due to its strategic location at the crossroads of South Asia, Central Asia, and the Middle East. Its proximity to Afghanistan, Iran and China makes it a major player of interest in the region. Pakistan has leveraged its strength to act as an important collaborator for the extraneous forces engaged in enduring great game in South Asia. This chapter focuses on the characteristics of Pakistan as a regional and strategic participant which not only impacts the future of Pakistan but also the overall security calculus in the region.

Factology

Pakistan, officially the Islamic Republic of Pakistan, is the fifth most populous country with a population exceeding 240 million people.[2] It is the 36th largest country in the world in terms of area with an area covering 881,913 Square kms. Pakistan has a 1,046 Km coastline along the Arabian Sea and the Gulf of Oman bordered by India to the east, Afghanistan to the west, Iran to the southwest and China in the far northeast respectively. It is separated from Tajikistan by Afghanistan's narrow Wakhan Corridor in the north and also shares a maritime border with Oman.

The territory that now constitutes Pakistan is considered a cradle of civilisation which was previously home to several ancient cultures, including the Mehrgarh of the Neolithic period and the Bronze Age Indus Valley

Civilization. It was later home to kingdoms ruled by people of different faiths and cultures, including Hindus, Indo-Greeks, Muslims, Turco-Mongols, Afghans and Sikhs. The area has been ruled by numerous empires and dynasties, including the Persian Achaemenid Empire, Alexander of Macedonia, the Arab Umayyad Caliphate, the Delhi Sultanate, the Mongol Empire, the Mughal Empire, the Durrani Empire, the Sikh Empire and the British Empire.

Pakistan is unique among Muslim countries as it is the only country to have been created in the name of Islam. As a result of the Pakistan movement led by Muhammad Ali Jinnah, Pakistan was created in 1947 as an independent nation for Muslims of the region in the east and west of the sub-continent. Initially a dominion, Pakistan adopted a new constitution in 1956, becoming an Islamic republic. A civil war in 1971 resulted in the secession of East Pakistan and creation of a new country of Bangladesh.

Pakistan's federal parliamentary republic consists of four provinces, one federal capital territory and two self-governing administrative territories. The four provinces are Punjab, Sindh, Khyber Pakhtunkhwa and Baluchistan. The Islamabad Capital Territory covers the capital city, while the Federally Administered Tribal Areas in the northwest including the Frontier Regions with Afghanistan were merged with Khyber Pakhtunkhwa in 2018. The two self-governing administrative territories are Pakistan Occupied Kashmir and Gilgit-Baltistan. The local governance system of Pakistan consists of three tiers viz. districts, tehsils (sub-districts) and union councils. Each tier has elected bodies. In total, there are approximately 149 districts, 588 tehsils and several thousand union councils.

Pakistan is an ethnically and linguistically diverse country, with a similar variation in its geography and wildlife. A regional and middle power, Pakistan Army is the sixth largest army in the world and the largest in the Muslim world. It is also a nuclear power with formidable nuclear arsenal. It has a semi- industrialized economy with a well-integrated agriculture sector. Its economy is the 24th largest in the world in terms of purchasing power and 46th largest in terms of nominal GDP.[3] Pakistan has a hierarchically structured court system with two classes of court, the superior and the subordinate judiciary. The superior judiciary is entrusted with preserving, protecting, and defending the constitution and comprises the Supreme Court of Pakistan, the

Federal Shariat Court and five High Courts. The Supreme Court stands at the apex, and one high court serves each province, with the last serving the Islamabad Capital Territory. Pakistan Occupied Kashmir and Gilgit-Baltistan have separate court systems. The subordinate judiciary consists of civil and criminal district courts.[4]

The post-independence history of Pakistan has been characterised by periods of military rule, political instability and conflicts with neighbouring India. The country continues to face challenging problems, including overpopulation, terrorism, economic duress, poverty, illiteracy, and corruption. Despite these factors, it maintains strategic endowments and developmental potential making itself relevant both at the regional and global level. Irrespective of the recent political turmoil and economic windfall, the nation has withstood the turbulent times and managed to remain afloat. It is a member of the United Nations, the Commonwealth of Nations, the Next Eleven Economies, Shanghai Cooperation Organisation (SCO), ECO, D8, Kyoto Protocol, ICCPR, RCD, UNCHR, Asian Infrastructure Investment Bank, Group of Eleven, CPFTA, Group of 24, the G20 developing nations, ECOSOC, founding member of the Organisation of Islamic Cooperation (OIC), SAARC and CERN.

Leveraging Factors

A number of factors lend distinct geo-strategic advantage to Pakistan as illustrated below:

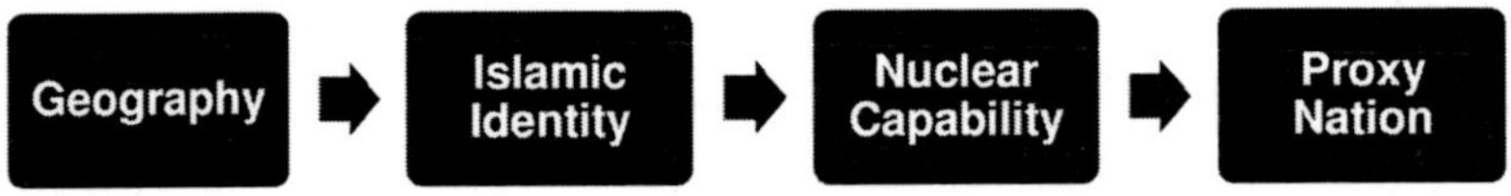

Geography. Pakistan is strategically located in the neighbourhood of China, Russia and India. It stands at the doorway of oil and energy rich countries of the Middle East and Central Asia, serving as an important conduit between diverse eco-systems of resource rich countries and dependent economies. US interests in the region have remained constant over many years. At an early stage, it patronized Pakistan to offset communist influence of Russia and later to seek its cooperation in the GWOT. The construction of CPEC as part of China's BRI has raised the stakes for China which seeks to secure access to the

Western waters through deep sea port of Gwadar. However, whether Pakistan would be able to leverage its strategic location in the future or not, is a moot question given the complexities of geo-strategy and economic interdependencies which are shaping the global environment today. Major advantages lend by the geography of Pakistan are elaborated below:

- **Access to Key Regions.** Pakistan's location bridges South Asia, Central Asia, and the Middle East. This makes it a key player in regional geopolitics and trade. The China-Pakistan Economic Corridor (CPEC) is a prime example of this significance, as it connects the Chinese city of Kashgar to Pakistan's Gwadar Port, providing China access to the Arabian Sea and subsequently, the Indian Ocean.[5]
- **Balancing Power Dynamics.** Pakistan's location serves as a balancing factor in the region's power dynamics. It shares borders with China, Afghanistan, India and Iran. Its strategic importance is evident in the way major world powers, such as the United States and Russia, have sought to engage with Pakistan to expand their interests in South and Central Asia. Pakistan's role in the Soviet Afghan War and subsequently the GWOT stands testimony to the strategic leverage provided by Pakistan in furthering the interest of western powers.
- **Ports and Trade Routes.** The port city of Karachi, located on the Arabian Sea, is Pakistan's largest and most important port, handling a major portion of the country's trade. It serves as a gateway for imports and exports, including oil shipments from the Middle East. The importance of Karachi has further increased due to its proximity to key global shipping lanes. Development of the Gwadar Port, located in the southwestern province of Baluchistan, provides Pakistan with a deep-sea port that offers strategic access to the Arabian Sea and the global maritime trade network. Gwadar is being developed with support from China under the CPEC, which will connect China's Xinjiang region to the Arabian Sea, further boosting Pakistan's economic and geopolitical significance.
- **Natural Resources.** Pakistan's Indus Valley, with its fertile soil, supports one of the world's most productive agricultural regions. The Indus River system, fed by the Himalayan and Karakoram Mountain

ranges, provides water for irrigation, making Pakistan a major producer of wheat, rice, cotton and other cash crops. The mountainous regions, particularly in the northern and southwestern parts of Pakistan, are rich in mineral resources, including coal, copper, gold, and natural gas. These resources contribute to the economic potential of the country. The rivers in Pakistan, particularly the Indus, provide substantial potential for hydroelectric power generation. Pakistan has developed several dams and hydroelectric plants to harness water resources for power generation, such as the Mangla and Tarbela dams. Pakistan's potential for hydropower is estimated at around 60,000 MW. However, only about 16% of this potential has been harnessed so far.

- **Military Advantage**. The mountainous terrain of the north (Himalayas and Hindu Kush ranges) serves as natural defence barriers, while the plains in the east facilitate mobilization and logistics. These natural barriers have helped Pakistan in protection against invasions and military aggression from the north. They also contain significant glacial resources, which provide water to the Indus River system. The strategic mountain passes, such as the Khyber Pass, historically served as key routes for invasions and trade between Central Asia and the Indian subcontinent. The control of such passes has given Pakistan an important geopolitical advantage.
- **Geographical Challenges**. Inspite of several opportunities provided by the unique geography of Pakistan, there are challenges which emanate from the peculiar location of the state that impacts security in the region. Pakistan shares borders with India, Afghanistan, Iran, and China. Pakistan's border with India and Afghanistan, in particular, are contentious marked by violence and continued military deployment. Pakistan is also prone to natural calamities which adversely impacts the predominant agrarian economy of the state.

Islamic Identity. The Islamic identity of Pakistan is central to the nation's formation, culture, politics and social fabric. It has shaped the country since its inception in 1947 and remains a key factor in its strategic calculus today. Key precepts of Pakistan's Islamic Identity are as under:

- **Pakistan's Constitution.** Pakistan's constitution adopted in 1973, declares Islam as the state religion.[6]

  The Constitution also emphasizes the importance of ensuring that all laws in Pakistan conform to Islamic principles. Article 2 of the Constitution states, "Islam shall be the State religion of Pakistan." The Constitution also incorporates Islamic principles in its legal framework, such as the establishment of the Sharia (Islamic law) in various aspects of governance, including family law and criminal law.
- **Islam Envisioned as a Unifying Force.** In a country with diverse ethnic, linguistic, and regional groups, Islam was envisioned as a unifying force for the people of Pakistan. Despite regional differences, Islam was to be the common thread that ties the nation together. However, today Pakistan is more divided than united by Islam. The state has endeavoured to promote a collective identity based on religious unity. Islamic scholars and religious leaders are shaping Pakistan's identity and influence political decisions, especially regarding the role of religion in state affairs.
- **Pakistan and Organization of Islamic Countries** (OIC). As a founding member of the OIC, which was established in September 1969, Pakistan has been at the forefront of the OIC's efforts to champion Muslim cause. Although Pakistan's initial attempts to create a pan-Islamist organization received a discouraging response from key Muslim states, Pakistan has tried to situate itself prominently within the OIC, evident in the active role it has taken within the organization. This activism is reflected in Islamabad's regular proposals to strengthen the OIC and its hosting of not just meetings but key OIC bodies.
- **Islamization as an Instrument of State Policy.** In the late 20th Century, especially during the military rule of General Zia-ul-Haq (1977–1988), Pakistan underwent a period of Islamization.[7] Zia's government implemented measures to align the state and society more closely with Islamic principles, including the introduction of stricter laws on Islamic dress, public morality and religious education. Political parties in Pakistan often draw upon Islam in their platforms. For instance, the Jamaat Ulema-e-Islam (JUI) and Pakistan Tehreek-e-

Insaf (PTI), led by Imran Khan, have emphasized the importance of establishing an 'Islamic welfare state' based on the teachings of the Quran and Sunnah (traditions of the Prophet Muhammad).

- **Islamic Social Welfare.** The primary aim of the Pakistani state, under its Islamic identity, has been to establish a welfare state based on Islamic teachings. This is reflected in the focus on charity, social justice and the elimination of poverty. Institutions like the Zakat (almsgiving) and Bait-ul-Mal (state fund for helping the needy) were designed to help the underprivileged in line with Islamic values. It is however strange that religion has become more of a political agenda in Pakistan instead of assuming the idealistic stature it was envisioned by the founding fathers of Pakistan.
- **Challenges to Islamic Identity.** The Islamic identity of Pakistan is deeply embedded in the nation's history, constitution, politics, and culture. It serves as a unifying force for the majority Muslim population, but it has also created challenges regarding religious pluralism and the treatment of minorities. There are tensions between different Islamic sects, particularly between Sunni and Shia Muslims. The nation's Islamic identity is a source of pride for many, yet it also continues to be a subject of debate and evolution within the context of global changes, internal politics, and regional dynamics. Pakistan has also faced challenges in managing extremism and terrorism, often in the name of Islam.

Nuclear Capability. Pakistan is one of the world's most sensitive nuclear-armed states. Pakistan's relevance as a nuclear state is multifaceted, extending far beyond military deterrence. Its nuclear weapons serve as a critical component of national security, particularly in the context of its rivalry with India and also provide the country with significant geopolitical leverage in South Asia as well as globally. While Pakistan's nuclear status has brought it a degree of international importance, it also places the country at the centre of debate on nuclear non-proliferation, arms control and global security. The stability of Pakistan's nuclear deterrent, the potential for nuclear escalation and its role in regional and global security are key issues that continue to shape Pakistan's foreign and defence policies. Important aspects of Pakistan's nuclear identity are elaborated below:

- **Historical Context.** The primary inspiration for Pakistan's nuclear weapons program was its longstanding rivalry with India. Since partition in 1947, India and Pakistan have fought four wars, with the Kashmir dispute being a central point of contention. India's nuclear weapons capability, developed in 1974, prompted Pakistan to pursue its own nuclear weapons as a deterrent to Indian military superiority.
- **Nuclear Deterrence.** Pakistan's nuclear weapons are viewed as a strategic deterrent to prevent India from using conventional military force against Pakistan, especially in the context of a potential escalation over Kashmir besides other issues. The concept of 'minimum credible deterrence' is central to Pakistan's nuclear doctrine, meaning that Pakistan aims to maintain a nuclear capability sufficient to deter aggression, without necessarily seeking to match India's nuclear arsenal in terms of size or sophistication.
- **Balance of Power in South Asia.** Pakistan's nuclear capability helps maintain a balance of power in South Asia, allegedly preventing the probability of any military adventurism. The presence of nuclear weapons on both sides has created a state of mutually assured destruction in the region which paradoxically may help to prevent full-scale wars between the two nuclear-armed nations.
- **Influence in South Asia.** Pakistan's status as a nuclear power enhances its influence in the South Asian region. It is often seen as a key player in regional security dynamics, particularly with regards to conflicts in Afghanistan and its strategic alliances, such as with China and the United States. Pakistan's nuclear status gives it leverage in diplomatic negotiations, regional security dialogues and international relations.
- **Nuclear Non-Proliferation Treaty (NPT).** Pakistan has not signed the NPT, which it views as discriminatory, given India's nuclear capabilities. As a non-signatory, Pakistan is often subject to international scrutiny, particularly from Western powers, which have concerns about nuclear proliferation and the security of Pakistan's nuclear arsenal.
- **International Relations.** Pakistan's nuclear status shapes its relations with major powers. Its nuclear capability has made it a critical ally of

China which views Pakistan as a counterbalance to India. On the other hand, Western nations, particularly the United States, have at times expressed concerns about Pakistan's nuclear weapons falling into the hands of non-state actors or extremists.

- **Nuclear Suppliers Group (NSG).** Pakistan's exclusion from the NSG, a group of countries that seek to control nuclear trade and prevent nuclear proliferation, highlights the global divide on nuclear proliferation. Pakistan has sought membership in the NSG, arguing that its nuclear program should be recognized to meet civilian nuclear technology requirements.
- **No First Use (NFU).** Unlike India, which has a declared NFU policy regarding nuclear weapons, Pakistan has not formally adopted NFU, making it more ambiguous in its nuclear posture. Pakistan's nuclear doctrine emphasizes the possibility of using nuclear weapons in response to a significant conventional attack, particularly in the case of an existential threat. This has raised concerns about the potential for nuclear escalation in the event of a conflict with India.
- **Tactical Nuclear Weapons (TNWs).** Pakistan has developed TNWs, which are lower-yield nuclear weapons designed for use on the battlefield rather than for deterrence at the strategic level. The development of these weapons has raised concerns about their potential use in a limited or localized conflict with India.
- **Safety of Nuclear Weapons.** One of the most significant international concerns regarding Pakistan's nuclear weapons is the security of its nuclear arsenal. Given the country's challenges with terrorism, extremism and political instability, there are fears that nuclear weapons could be vulnerable to theft or misuse by non-state actors. Pakistan has consistently assured the world that its nuclear weapons are under strict control and that there is no risk of them falling into the hands of extremists, which seems suspect.
- **Civilian Nuclear Energy.** Beyond military applications, Pakistan also uses its nuclear technology for civilian purposes, particularly in generating electricity. Pakistan's nuclear power plants play a role in addressing the country's energy needs, reducing its dependency on

fossil fuels. However, civilian nuclear energy development is closely tied to the country's overall nuclear infrastructure, raising concerns about potential dual-use technology.

Proxy Nation. Despite intractable challenges and discordant forces Pakistan has always managed to stay afloat. Pakistan has been able to exploit various leverages to remain relevant, whether it was playing up the perennial belligerence against India or its support to the US in GWOT. The support of its all-weather friend China is another important factor which has not allowed Pakistan to fail as a state in the past. Metaphorically Pakistan can be compared to a prawn which doesn't have any guts, no spine, has a useless head, but still gets its value in the market irrespective of everything that is negative about its existence. It's intriguing therefore to study the oscillating behaviour of Pakistan in terms of its relations with US and China specifically and the comity of Islamic nations in general which has enabled it to survive through apparently unsurmountable challenges.

- **Pakistan-US Relations.** Over the years, Pakistan-US relationship has fluctuated, with periods of increased cooperation followed by tensions. Despite these challenges, US has continued to provide military and financial aid to Pakistan. Balancing shared interests while addressing mutual concerns remains a critical aspect of this enduring partnership. Pakistan has benefited from its relationship with the US in several ways:
    - ✓ **Economic Aid and Investment.** The US has been a significant source of development aid, supporting programs in education, health, and infrastructure. Additionally, the US is Pakistan's largest export market, providing favourable access for Pakistani goods.
    - ✓ **Military and Security Cooperation.** Pakistan has received military aid and equipment from the US, enhancing its defence capabilities. The two countries have also cooperated on counterterrorism efforts and border security.
    - ✓ **Educational Opportunities.** The US has facilitated educational exchanges through programs like the Fulbright Scholarship, allowing many Pakistanis to study in the US. This has helped build a strong foundation of people-to-people ties.

- ✓ **Technological and Medical Assistance.** The US has supported Pakistan in various technological and medical fields, including the provision of COVID-19 vaccines and building detection and treatment capacities.
- ✓ **Strategic Alliances.** Historically, Pakistan has played a crucial role in facilitating US interests in the region, such as during the Cold War and the War on Terror. Despite the ups and downs in their relationship, these benefits have contributed to Pakistan's development and regional stability.

- **Pakistan-China Friendship.** The China-Pakistan relationship is multifaceted and has evolved over several decades, shaped by political, economic, military and strategic considerations. The Pakistan-China friendship, often described as 'higher than the Himalayas, deeper than the oceans', is the foundation of Pakistan's foreign policy.[8] The solid strategic and economic partnership between the two countries has strengthened over the years, with China investing significantly in Pakistan's infrastructure and development. Beyond economics, both countries have also collaborated closely on regional diplomacy. This strategic partnership serves mutual interests, including countering regional challenges and enhancing their geopolitical influence in South Asia and beyond. Key aspects of the China-Pakistan relationship are listed below:
  - ✓ **Historical Background.** The China-Pakistan relationship began in the early 1950s, shortly after the creation of Pakistan and the establishment of the People's Republic of China. Over time, they developed close diplomatic ties, particularly after the 1960s. Both countries have shared interests in countering India influence in the region. China has been a long-standing supporter of Pakistan's territorial claims, including on the Kashmir issue.
  - ✓ **Strategic and Military Cooperation.** China has been a key supplier of military equipment to Pakistan including fighter jets, tanks, and submarines. The two countries have collaborated on various defence projects, including the development of missile systems. Today almost 80% of equipment in Pakistan Armed

Forces is of Chinese origin.

- ✓ **Border Security.** Both countries share a border in the western region, with China's Xinjiang province bordering Pakistan's Gilgit-Baltistan. The two nations coordinate closely on issues of border security, especially against separatist and terrorist activities.
- ✓ **Counterterrorism Cooperation.** Pakistan and China have also cooperated on counterterrorism efforts, with China playing a role in supporting Pakistan's operations in its restive regions.
- ✓ **Economic Ties.** One of the most significant aspects of Pakistan-China relationship is the CPEC, a vast infrastructure project that aims to connect China's Xinjiang region to Pakistan's Gwadar port. CPEC is a key part of China's Belt and Road Initiative (BRI) and involves investments in infrastructure, energy projects, and transportation networks. The total investment in CPEC is expected to exceed $60 billion, making it a cornerstone of the bilateral relationship.
- ✓ **Trade.** China is Pakistan's largest trading partner, and trade between the two countries has grown significantly over the years. Both countries have signed free trade agreements and have been working to increase economic exchanges in sectors like agriculture, textiles, and technology.
- ✓ **Energy Projects.** China has invested heavily in Pakistan's energy sector, especially in power plants and renewable energy projects. This is crucial for Pakistan, which faces significant energy shortages.
- ✓ **Diplomatic Relations.** China and Pakistan work closely within regional forums such as the SCO. Pakistan supports China's stand on issues like Taiwan and Xinjiang, while China has supported Pakistan's position on Kashmir in international forums. China has been an important ally for Pakistan in international organizations such as the United Nations, often vetoing resolutions that Pakistan sees as unfavourable, especially on the Kashmir issue.

- ✓ **Geopolitical Implications.** The China-Pakistan alliance has implications for the broader South Asian region, especially in relation to India. India views the growing Sino-Pakistan cooperation as a threat to its security and regional dominance. The strategic partnership between China and Pakistan has fuelled India's concerns about encirclement and regional balance of power.
- ✓ **Cultural and Educational Exchanges.** There is increasing cooperation in terms of educational exchanges with more Pakistani students studying in China. Additionally, both countries share cultural ties, particularly in areas like traditional medicine, language, and art. Military exchanges between the two countries in terms of orientation and training has also witnessed surge in the recent years.
- ✓ **Tourism and Diplomacy.** As bilateral relations have improved, people-to-people exchanges have also grown between Pakistan and China, although the volume is not as high as it could be. Both sides are:

- **Guardian Angels.** The third most important factor which has kept the country going are the so-called guardian angels which are countries that have greater interest in Pakistan. Saudi Arabia has been cultivating Pakistan to remain a hegemon in Muslim world and so has been the reason for Turkey cozying up to Pakistan. While the US desires to prevent Pakistan from falling into the Chinese hands, China on the other hand nurtures and supports Pakistan to develop it as a proxy against India. Islam is another glue which Pakistan has exploited to repeatedly seek favours from Islamic nations. Being the only Islamic country to possess nuclear weapons, Pakistan often champions its nuclear capability amidst Islamic fraternity, to underline its importance.

Pakistan's Strategic Conundrum

Having reviewed the geo-strategic importance of Pakistan it is prudent to analyze the strategic viewpoint of Pakistan which has evolved through several shades from the times of its birth. The foundational influences of Pakistan's strategic behaviour are drawn from the impact of partition, secondly from the perpetuation of beliefs in an Islamic military exceptionalism and thirdly from the impact of the 1947/48 Indo-Pakistan War. Convergence of these three elements laid the foundation of a Pakistan strategic culture with the Pakistan Army Officer Corps being its primary initiator. Closely aligned to this is the idea of a vengeful India, the need for strategic depth and concomitant need for a pliant Afghanistan which has shaped the behaviour of Pakistan. [9]

The study of strategic culture focuses on the historical experiences and narratives of the policymakers, their perceptions of the adversary's intentions and capabilities, and the challenges they encounter in their interaction with the rest of the world, especially the immediate neighbours. The fact that Pakistan was a new state, carved out of India on the basis of Muslim separatism, has contributed to its insecurity. Most Indians, especially the policymakers, viewed the establishment of Pakistan as a negation of the principles they stood for during the struggle for independence. Their disposition towards Pakistan ranged from reluctant acceptance to a hope that the new state might collapse, making it possible for the separated territories to return to India. Pakistani leaders overemphasized their separateness and distinct identity reacting sharply to what they perceived as India's attempts to strangle the new state in its infancy.

The military plays a dominant role in Pakistan's strategic culture, both in terms of policy formulation and national security priorities. The Pakistan Army, due to its prominence in shaping the nation's political and foreign policy, has a deep influence on strategic decisions. The military leadership's worldview, particularly its focus on defence and deterrence, is a critical factor in how Pakistan views regional security. Pakistan's military has historically been able to exert significant control over political institutions, even leading the country during multiple military coups. This has contributed to a strategic culture where the military is seen as the primary institution responsible for safeguarding the nation's interests and addressing perceived threats.

Pakistan's wars with India have significantly impacted her strategic behaviour leaving an indelible mark on its identity and character. Enchantment with Kashmir and high-headed authoritarian outlook towards its Eastern Wing led to permanent mutilation of Pakistan drastically altering the form with which it was created at partition. The scars of 1971 have embellished the national conscience of Pakistan which they perceive as an unfair and cunning conspiracy by India. Pakistan's role in the Russia-Afghan conflict and its exuberance in setting up the Mujahideen factory gave birth to an eco system which has become a challenge for her today. The animal that was propped up as an instrument of state policy and leverage against India has turned around and started biting the hand that fed it. All these events of history with misgivings and disappointments have contributed in the evolution of the strategic outlook that has been adopted by Pakistan.

Islam has been integral to Pakistan's strategic culture because it contributes to shaping societal dispositions and the orientations of the policymakers. Islam is closely associated with the establishment of the state and the constitution designates the state as an Islamic Republic with a stipulation that no law can be enacted that violates the basic principles and teachings of Islam. Islam figures prominently in political and military discourse. All political parties with some popular standing recognize the centrality of Islam to the political process and highlight their commitment to Islam in their election manifestos and policy statements. Education at the primary, secondary, and college levels (the first 14 years of education) includes Islamic studies (principles and teachings of Islam) as a compulsory course of study at all levels for Muslim students. The historical narratives highlight the advent of Islam in India, glorify Muslim rule and define Pakistani identity with reference to Islam and the Muslim rule. These narratives also maintain that the Muslim interests and rights were threatened by an unsympathetic Hindu majority during the British rule, forcing the Muslims to first seek constitutional safeguards and then a separate state. If Islamic orientations and values are so deeply rooted in the society and the state, these are bound to influence the strategic culture of Pakistan.

The major features of Pakistan's strategic culture can be summarized to include:

- An acute insecurity developed in the early years of independence due to troubled relations with India and problems with Afghanistan.
- A strong distrust of India and a history of acrimonious Indo-Pakistani relations reinforced by the historical narratives of the pro-independence period and the troubled bilateral interaction in the post-independence period.
- Pakistan perceives itself as an insecure and incomplete state, which

drives its efforts to secure its borders and maintain a strong military presence.

- Aversion to an India-dominated regional power arrangement for South Asia.
- An active search for security to maintain its independence in deciding about foreign policy options and domestic policies.
- A close nexus between Islam and strategic thinking, leading to connections between Islamic militancy and foreign policy.
- Pakistan believes that Afghanistan is a source of instability and seeks to exert influence there to create a buffer zone against potential threats, particularly from India.
- Pakistan views India as a regional hegemon that seeks to dominate or destroy it. This perception has led to a focus on countering India's influence and maintaining a balance of power.
- Pakistan has historically used proxy fighters to achieve its strategic objectives, particularly in regions like Kashmir. This strategy is seen as a way to counterbalance India's conventional military superiority.
- Pakistan's strategic culture includes a strong emphasis on nuclear deterrence as a means to ensure its security and prevent external aggression.

Pakistan's strategic behaviour is dictated by a complex blend of historical experiences, military priorities, regional dynamics, ideological considerations and external alliances. Its approach to security is heavily influenced by its rivalry with India, the legacy of partition, the need for deterrence and the desire for geopolitical relevance. The ibid attributes of Pakistan's strategic culture have shaped her security and foreign policy options which critically influences the geo-political environment in the region and security in South Asia. While nuclear deterrence and military capabilities are central, Pakistan also employs unconventional methods, such as proxy warfare, to strengthen its position. Its relationship with China, the US and the Middle East further influences its strategic decisions. Ultimately, Pakistan's strategic culture is marked by pragmatism and a constant balancing act between external threats and internal challenges deeply influenced by the course of critical events in its history.

Conclusion

The geo-strategic importance of Pakistan cannot be emphasized enough for of reasons as discussed in this section. A revisionist state, Pakistan was never content with partition and has repeatedly challenged the Status Quo seeking leverage of its geography and greater influence in the region. Meandering its course through turbulent waters internally, Pakistan has championed its position to remain attractive to the global players (predominantly US and China in the current context). The fault lines of the state and its future trajectory will hinge on the strategic choices made by Pakistan's power centres, shaping the broader security and strategic landscape of the region.

Notes

1 Stephen P. Cohen, 2004, "The Idea of Pakistan", Washington, D.C.: Brookings Institution Press.
2 "Pakistan Center for South Asian and Middle Eastern Studies Illinois," n.d., https://csames.illinois.edu/sas/sa-resources/countries/pakistan.
3 "Pakistan Overview", https://www.worldbank.org.
4 "Pakistan Federal System", https://www.forumfed.org.
5 "CPEC", https://www.britannica.com.
6 "Constitution of Pakistan", https://na.gov.pk.
7 Md Ziaul Haque Sheikh, (2020), "Military, Authoritarianism and Islam", Cambridge Press.
8 Jeremy Garlick (2021), "Reconfiguring the China-Pakistan Economic Corridor", Routledge.
9 Mark Briskey, "The Foundation of Pakistan's Strategic Culture", https://www.usmcu.edu/

Chapter Three

The Fault Lines

"The Pakistani state is strong in some ways and extremely weak in others – its greatest threat is not India, but internal disintegration."

—**Anatol Lieven**[1]

Pakistan is an intriguing country. Envisioned as an exclusive homeland for the Muslims of Indian sub-continent, the religious glue was expected to hold the country together irrespective of social and ethnic divisions. Breaking away of East Pakistan with creation of Bangladesh in 1971 shattered this mirage of Muslim Nationalism revealing chinks in the very idea of Pakistan. These infirmities and many more which have manifested post creation of the state places a question mark on the future trajectory of Pakistan besides precipitating an environment of perennial instability in the region.

This chapter dwells upon major fault lines in Pakistan as relevant from India's perspective. One may feel that every crisis in Pakistan creates a potential hazard for India. While these developments would concern India, qualifying it as a threat would be incorrect and alarmist. In the same breath, it must also be acknowledged that regardless of the severity or complexity of the situation, Pakistan has repeatedly demonstrated the capability to rescue itself from any catastrophe much to the surprise and disbelief of larger global community. The very fact that Pakistan has managed to remain afloat amidst perpetual environment of chaos necessitates a pragmatic assessment and study of precarious fault lines.

Identity: The Critical Fault line

Identity of any nation is multifaceted, shaped by historical events, cultural diversity, political dynamics and social challenges. But Pakistan is a different ball game. Steered by the ambition of few in Muslim League, the idea of Pakistan was intended to be an argument to rally Muslim votes rather than a genuine call for a separate nation. Religious rhetoric was an important part of the strategy of Muslim League as this was an effective tool to gather diverse range of people on one platform, which succeeded politically to a large extent. The Muslims of the subcontinent otherwise had little in common. The thought of a homogeneous Muslim identity had been toyed earlier, firstly in 1930 by Iqbal in his famous Allahabad address and later by Choudhry Rahmat Ali who published a pamphlet called 'Now or Never' at Cambridge in 1933, although the realistic aspiration for Pakistan did not consolidate till elections of 1945.[2] These elections were an opportunity for Muslim League to amalgamate the Muslim votes stamping the authority of Muslim League as the legitimate voice of the community. The election rhetoric delivered the success desired by Muslim League but also gave momentum to the demand for a separate Pakistan state. At that stage neither the Congress nor the Muslim League was sure that British would cede to the demand for partition, which eventually came as a bit of surprise to both.

There were multiple factors which compelled British to leave India. Second World War had broken the back of the empire which was struggling to maintain the colony in Indian sub-continent. The rising influence of two prominent political parties in India besides the operations of Indian National Army under Subhash Chandra Bose had badly shaken the confidence of crown in India, forcing them to depart in hurry. Elated with success in 1945 elections wherein Muslim League secured a staggering 87% of the reserved Muslim seats, the political idea of Muslim identity had consolidated.[3] The Cabinet Mission Plan had failed in selling the idea of a united India, mainly due to the objections from Muslim League. Finally, amidst rising communal tensions, disagreement between the Congress and Muslim League and British desperation, the demand for a separate Pakistan state was finally accepted leading to one of the largest migrations of population in the recent history, soaked in blood and violence. Pakistan was created not with the ingredients of an ideal nation state but on the premise of an imaginary Muslim homeland desired by few but adopted by all. The two-nation theory finally succeeded in creating a geostrategic wedge between the Radcliffe and Durand Line, which simultaneously connected the oil rich Middle East, Soviet Central Asia, Chinese controlled East Turkestan, Tibet and the rest of the subcontinent.

Geoffrey Barraclough (2007) explains the process adopted by Pakistan to define national identity which takes place in roughly three stages.[4] The first stage was re-examination of indigenous culture wherein the religious clergy, local Muslim leaders and poets made an effort to go back to their culture and religion. The clergy called for a revival of true Islamic values while Iqbal revived the success stories of the ancestors of the Muslims in the subcontinent. The second stage, which is the new leadership, was also accurate in Pakistan where Pakistan saw leaders in the form of Syed Ahmed Khan who was responsible for invigorating a new generation of educated Muslims in the beginning of the 20th century. Jinnah provided leadership to gather masses on one platform first against the British and then for a separate country. The third stage is the mobilization of the masses which involved making sure the message of leaders and influencers percolates down to each and every Muslim in India, uniting them for a common legislated cause. Pakistan quite accurately passed through all the three stages mentioned by Barraclough. However, the problem was that the narrative of exploiting religious sentiments of Muslims in the sub-continent did not extend beyond 1947. Muslim League succeeded to get a separate piece of land but since the differences between the Muslims that made up Pakistan were so stark and vivid, the common religious thread could ever bind them together effectively. After the state of Pakistan was created, there was no genuine effort to build up a national narrative which would be inclusive and participative. Rather an 'ideology' based on myths was propagated which remains a faultline till today.

Pakistan has never exhibited a monolithic national identity. The geographical region that came to constitute Pakistan was more disjointed than integrated at multiple levels. According to the 2017 Census, 96.4% of Pakistanis identified as Muslims. However, within the followers of Islamic faith there are divisions between Sunnis, Shias, Imamiyyas, Ismaili and Bohras. The Sunnis further follow different schools of practice to include Barelvis, Deobandis, Hanfis, Maliki, Shafii, Hanbali etc. Followers of these different faiths are mostly antagonistic to each other lacking tolerance and compatibility. Today in times of economic uncertainty and rising social discontent, religion is increasingly becoming frictional, failing to define the national identity of Pakistan. Another dissonance faced by Pakistan is the fact that India which has a sizeable strength of Muslim continues to cohabitate peacefully with the majority Hindu population which was proclaimed as an impossibility by the proponents of Pakistan. On the other hand, East Pakistan with a predominant Muslim population was expected to align successfully with the all-encompassing idea of religious contiguity, got separated from Pakistan due to political and social repudiation. Rightfully so, religion has proven to be an incorrect constituent of national identity much to the chagrin of standard bearers of the very idea of Pakistan.

Another important facet of Pakistan's flawed identity is the professed belligerence against India and everything that India represents. It started with the cynical jockeying for power between Jawahar Lal Nehru and Mohammad Ali Jinnah, leading to partition although cultural friction between the two major communities of Indian subcontinent was nothing new. As J Sai Deepak mentions in his book 'India, Bharat and Pakistan: The Constitutional Journey of a Sandwiched Nation', Islamic colonization had significantly impacted the Indian region from eighth century onwards, primarily due to the inherent differences between Indic faiths and the beliefs of Middle Eastern Islamic traditions, which he describes as a form of 'coloniality' distinct from European colonialism; essentially suggesting that the spread of Islam in India was not just a religious conversion but also a process of cultural and political domination based on a perceived incompatibility between the two belief systems.[5] This perceived lack of incompatibility was exploited by the powers to be in Pakistan right from the early years with pompous display of flawed nationalism. The idea of Pakistan was marketed as a necessity to secure the interest and safety of Muslims against a belligerent Hindu nation. This narrative has repeatedly been exploited by the polity and specifically the Army in Pakistan to galvanize public opinion while securing endorsement for their rampant abuse of power.

False pretext of 'Islam in Danger' has been exploited for long to define Pakistan's identity. Pakistan has been feeding its population fabricated history of Islamic domination which was never visible in the region which came to be known as Pakistan. The area constituting Pakistan, for millennia has been the heart of 'India', full of rich heritage in the form of old architecture, culture and language. Pakistan's professed history begins with the attack of Mohammad Bin Qasim in 712 CE on Raja Dahir's Sind.[6] Pakistan has discredited the cultural ownership over Bappa Rawal (after whom Rawalpindi has been named), Lavapur (the original name of Lahore – named after the Son of Lord Ram, Lav), the ancient university of Taxila and even the genius of Indus Valley civilization. The extent of false indoctrination can be assed from an alleged signboard in Urdu erected at the ruins of Mohenjo-Daro stating that this is what Allah does to people who do not follow his true path.[7] As per this thought process everything was supposed to be 'Jahiliyyah' or the 'age of ignorance' before the advent of Islam, hence nothing good could have ever existed before that. This selective process of weaving a professed identity has not served the purpose as desired, leaving much to question.

Pakistan's attempt to create an artificial narrative starts early from schools and other institutions of education. Textbook of 10th grade printed by Pakistan's federal board of education states that Pakistan was created in 712 CE when the first Muslim in India, Muhammad Bin Qasim invaded the sub-continent. This statement is significant as it demonstrates attempts to shape public opinion regarding the roots of Muslim nationalism in India. Calling an Arab conqueror who invaded India in 712 CE as the 'first Pakistani' is a desperate attempt to seek endorsement of an Islamic character in an otherwise hybrid history of Indic faiths. This should mean that all subsequent Muslim invaders and rulers in India were also Pakistanis and contributed to the Muslim nationalism which later metamorphosed into Pakistani nationalism. But this is not the case, and a prime example of it is Mughal emperor Akbar who ruled India from 1556 till 1605. He is treated with disdain by the same narrative that shows Qasim as a hero. The reason being, Akbar was not really fond of the religious clergy and had brought Islam into an overly pluralistic disposition. The rational understanding of his actions was to garner the support and loyalty of the big non-Muslim population under his rule.

If we read the neutral authors and historians, there is a totally different picture that emerges. The Muslim invaders in India took pride in their language and regional lineages instead of the religion Islam. They also recruited people from similar ethnicities. A common cause of distrust amongst various invaders was different ethnicities and backgrounds who always tried to overthrow each other. There is no evidence of Muslims sharing a united nationhood based on the Islamic faith before the 19th century. On the contrary, at times, the divisions were encouraged by the rulers for political gains. The Muslim invaders in the subcontinent invoked the Muslim sentiment during war and invasions. However, when they were ruling, they suppressed the clergy as an absolute rule of religion or Sharia would have proved detrimental to their reign and would have brought the clergy to power. Historically speaking Pakistan identifying with invading Muslims is the biggest flaw in the quest for crafting a national identity in Pakistan.

Imposition of Urdu as the national language of Pakistan was another attempt to adopt uniformity in the country. Urdu, the lingua franca of Pakistan, imported from the courts of Mughal and Awadh rulers is sparsely spoken in regions other than Punjab. The proponents of Urdu did not take into account the fact that cultures that composed Pakistan were extremely proud of their language and unique identity which would not accept this diktat so easily. The strange part was that Urdu was rarely spoken is regions of Sindh, Baluchistan, FATA (later Khyber Pakhtunkhwa) and most prominently not in East Pakistan which was separated from Bengal. Urdu was the language in Muslim minority regions of undivided India which the new state of Pakistan could never associate with. The irony is that Urdu is not the native language of any of the four key native ethnic groups of Pakistan. Urdu as mother tongue was spoken by only 60% of those who migrated to Pakistan from India which makes it just about 5% of the total population of Pakistan.[8] Urdu therefore doesn't play any role in fostering a Cultural National Identity for Pakistan as it is being spoken by 95% Pakistanis as a second language just because it has the endorsement of the government. Most of the Pakistanis resent the importance Urdu enjoys in power corridors of the state and regard it as a foreign language.

As per Tilak Devasher, a prominent voice on Pakistan, four instruments have been used to forge a common identity in Pakistan viz. religion, centralization, Urdu and a perennial threat from India.[9] All these instruments are fraught with inconsistencies and do not hold favour in logic or acceptance within common conscious of Pakistan. Resultantly the dispensation in power appears to be constantly in an overdrive mode in enforcing these instruments which has created more incongruence rather than uniting the Pakistanis. After independence from the British, there were two paths that could have been taken by Pakistan. The first one was commitment towards nation building, strengthening democratic institutions for inclusive and participatory democracy, recognizing the ethnically, socially and culturally diverse groups and building a new country. This path would have been taken if Pakistan's leadership had realized that the 'two nation theory' had outlived itself once the country was created. The second path was dependent on continuous flogging of the 'two nation theory' to repeatedly reinforce its importance in defining homogenous Pakistani national identity. The raison d'être of Pakistan has been 'not being India'. Unfortunately, Pakistan has chosen to follow the latter path.

Religion and Ideology: The Contrived Faultline

> *"Minorities, to whichever community they may belong, will be safeguarded. Their religion or faith or belief will be secure. There will be no interference of any kind with their freedom of worship. They will have their protection with regard to their religion, faith, their life, their culture. They will be, in all respects, the citizens of Pakistan without any distinction of caste or creed. They will have their rights and privileges and no doubt, along with it goes the obligation of citizenship. Therefore, the minorities have their responsibilities also and they will play their part in the affairs of this state. As long as the minorities are loyal to the State and owe true allegiance and as long as I have any power, they need have no apprehension of any kind."*
>
> **—Mohammad Ali Jinnah**[10]

What was Pakistan meant to be? For Jinnah it was to be a secular democratic republic with a Muslim majority population as evident from the above statement given by him during a press conference on 14 Jul 1947. For the Ulema it was to be an Islamic republic following the Sharia. For the general Muslims it was to be a safe haven, less for their own advancement. It is surprising that Islam has remained a concept much abused by the political and religious leaders and leveraged effectively by the established wielding power and influence. As Sushant Sareen, a senior Research Fellow and author says, strategic overreach (punching way above its weight) coupled with perverse religiosity (especially in affairs of state and its ideology) have brought Pakistan to a pass where all its latent fault lines are virulently manifesting themselves, in the most dangerous proportion.

Religion plays a very important and significant role in Pakistan's society. But the moot question is does it integrate Pakistan's society or divide it? This is especially more important in a scenario wherein the cultural and social divide between the various provinces is so distinct and prominent. The constitution of Pakistan establishes Islam as the state religion but provides every citizen the right to profess, practice, and propagate his religion subject to law, public order and morality.[11] As per US Commission on International Religious Freedom (USCIRF), 96.5% of Pakistan's population is Muslim.[12] The majority of Muslims in Pakistan practice Sunni Islam, while a minority are Shias. The remaining 3.5% of Pakistan's population is made up of Hindus, Christians, Sikhs, Buddhists, Bahais and Zoroastrians. Religion which was intended to be the overarching factor of identity and integration, today divides Pakistani society more than anything else.

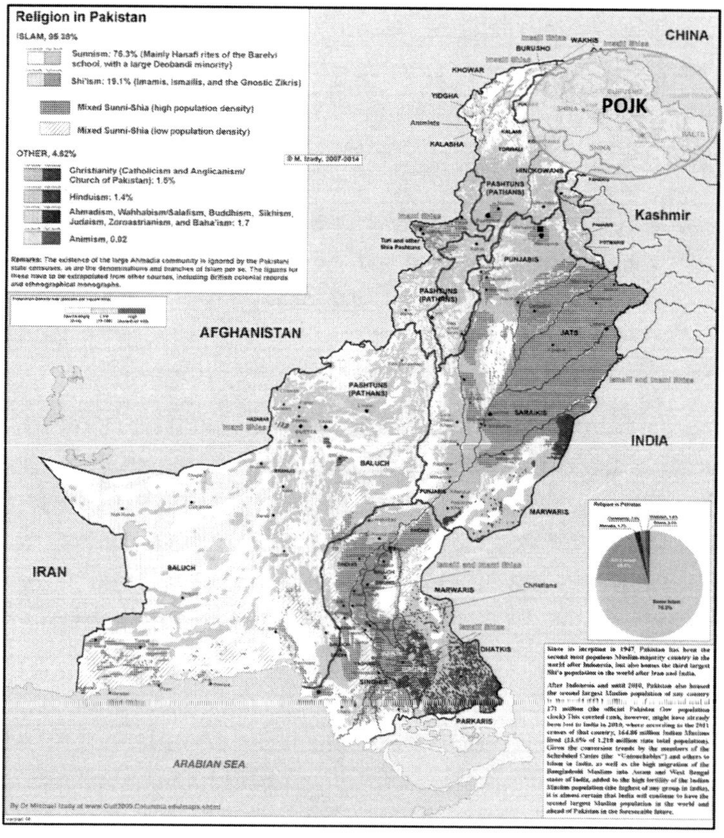

Fig 3.1: Sectarian Landscape in Pakistan[15]

Before talking about the fissures within practioners of Islam, it would be prudent to audit the status of religious minorities in Pakistan. According to the 2017 census of Pakistan, Hindus constitute 1.6% of Pakistan's population, followed by 1.59% Christians, 0.22% Ahmadis (Pakistan's constitution considers Ahmadis as non- Muslims), and 0.07% other minorities.[13] Status and treatment of Ahmadis has been discussed separately in the subsequent paras. Hindus mainly live in Sindh province and Christians in Punjab, whereas Ahmadis are evenly spread throughout the country. Most of the religious minorities in Pakistan live in rural areas. Although Articles 20, 21, 22, 25, 26 and 36 of the Constitution ensure equal rights of minorities without discrimination, there are numerous examples of injustices that are committed against them on an almost daily basis across the country.[14]

The discrimination against religious minorities in Pakistan has its roots in Pakistan's establishment, which was motivated based on religion. Rights of minorities in Pakistani were further curbed under the regime of General Zia-ul-Haq in the 1980s when the country was engineered towards Islamization for radicalization. The Islamization efforts also added prejudice, discrimination and structural violence against religious minorities. Religious minorities are frequently subjected to attacks and threats, targeted killings, lynching, mob violence, forced conversions, sexual violence against women and girls and desecration of places of worship and cemeteries. Increased space for radical Islamic groups in Pakistan has further accentuated intolerance against non-Muslims.

In addition to social intolerance, minorities face persecution of a more threatening kind, being accused of blasphemy. Blasphemy laws restrict any speech or action against Islam. Since their inception, these laws have been widely misused against minorities. In 1980s, General Zia-ul-Haq inserted eight sections (Sections 295, 295-A, 295-B, 295-C, 298, 298-A, 298-B, and 298-C) in Pakistan Penal Code under his Islamization agenda, commonly known as blasphemy laws.[16] Anyone who insults Islam, Islamic personalities, Muslim's holy book or religious feelings of Muslims can be declared blasphemous. However, the laws are vague as there is no clear definition of an act of blasphemy. These laws carry fine, jail sentence, life imprisonment and death penalty. If a person is accused, majority of the times they will be persecuted, and have fewer chances of getting justice. Anyone can accuse another individual of blasphemy, and he/she has no obligation to provide witness/proof in the court as repeating the 'allegation' itself is considered blasphemy. These laws are often used and exploited as a weapon of revenge against non-Muslims to settle personal scores or to resolve disputes over money, property, business etc. To give an example in the month of August 2020 alone, at least 42 blasphemy cases were registered against Shia Muslims across Pakistan.[17] Asia Bibi's case is a prime example of the misuse of these laws. Both Punjab Governor, Salman Taseer, a progressive Muslim and Federal Minister for Minority Affairs, was assassinated for speaking up for her. On 03 December 2021, a Sri Lankan citizen named Priyantha Kumara Diyawadana, was accused of blasphemy by Muslim labourers of a local factory in Sialkot, Punjab province, where he worked as a manager. He was lynched by the mob, and later his body was put on fire.[18]

Apart from other forms of violence, the number of forced conversion cases of girls are also rapidly increasing in Pakistan. It has been estimated by the Movement for Solidarity and Peace in Pakistan that every year about 1,000 Hindu and Christian girls, of which some are minors are abducted and forcefully converted to Islam.[19] Many of these girls are sexually exploited and then abandoned. These 'converts' can never return home or rejoin their original faith as apostasy is a crime punishable by death. So far, there are no laws or procedures put in place against these crimes in the country that makes minority girls more vulnerable and constant targets of abuse. Marginalised girls are sexually abused but accusers never get punished. Unfortunately, the state institutions have failed to protect them.

Hate speeches is another method of proliferating hatred against the minorities. Misinformation and derogatory comments are often used through media, including social media, in religious and public settings. State institutions are silent on this trend. Doctored school curriculum plays a critical role in intensifying intolerance against minorities. A study conducted by the Sustainable Development Policy Institute of Pakistan has pointed out that school textbooks are a major contributor in creating an environment of vitiated hate against the minorities by presenting a distorted version of national history.[20] The views in these textbooks encourage prejudice and bigotry towards women and religious minorities, glorify war and incite violence. Religious minorities in Pakistan continue to face a difficult and often hostile environment, with many facing discrimination, violence, and legal challenges.

Religious intolerance against the Ahmadis in Pakistan is something which is unimaginable. The Ahmadis consider themselves Muslim, but mainstream Sunni and Shia Muslims do not recognize them as such. In 1974, Pakistan officially declared Ahmadis as non-Muslims through a constitutional amendment.[21] Ahmadis face severe social and legal discrimination. They are prohibited from calling themselves Muslims, using Islamic greetings or engaging in any practice considered Islamic. The community members have also complained that they are routinely stopped from burying their deceased in the local cemeteries. There are several instances of deceased bodies being exhumed, sometimes under police orders, on the pretext of improper burial in a Muslim graveyard. In a notable incident on 06 December 2012, in Model Town, Lahore, 15 armed men vandalized and destroyed over 120 graves belonging to the Ahmadiyya community.[22] Many persons have been murdered after branding Ahmadis as 'Wajibul Qatl' (liable to be killed) creating an atmosphere of fear and insecurity. As per National Commission for Human Rights, between 1984 and 2023, 280 Ahmadis have lost their lives due to targeted violence and an additional 415 have faced assaults because of their faith. The assault on the religious identity of Ahmadis is evident in the demolition of 51 Ahmadiyya worship places and sealing of 46 others by authorities during the same period, revealing a systematic effort to ostracise the community.[23] Bitterness against Ahmadis is a typical characteristic of the Pakistani society which reflects deeply embedded hatred for the alleged non-believers.

The Sunni-Shia divide in Pakistan is another source of sectarian friction which has impacted the religious landscape in Pakistan. The conflict is primarily rooted in historical, theological and political dissent with each side taking a rigid and irreconcilable position. Sectarian identity and politics started right from the time Pakistan was created in 1947. The political elite at the time were predominantly Sunni, who created an environment of Sunni domination and its interpretation of Islam across the country. Marginalization of Shia practices, festivals and rituals in the state further compounded this divide. A major factor in the Sunni-Shia conflict in Pakistan has been the broader geopolitical rivalry between Sunni-majority Saudi Arabia and Shia-majority Iran. Under General Zia-ul-Haq, Sunni Islam became even more closely tied to state policies. Zia promoted a stricter interpretation of Sunni Islam, which alienated the Shia population and increased sectarian tensions. His regime's support for the Afghan Jihad against the Soviet Union also saw the introduction of more radical Sunni militancy into the country. There are also internal Sunni divisions, particularly between Deobandi and Barelvi sects, but these tend to align with broader Sunni-Shia tensions when it comes to political and religious expression.

Extremist groups like Sipah-e-Sahaba Pakistan (SSP), which is a Sunni extremist group and Lashkar-e-Jhangvi (LeJ), have targeted Shia Muslims, particularly in regions like Karachi, Quetta, and Gilgit-Baltistan. Over the years, numerous Shia leaders, intellectuals, and activists have been assassinated by Sunni extremist groups, leading to growing fear and anger within the Shia community. The Ashura (10th of Muharram) processions, which is central to Shia identity, have been frequently targeted with sectarian violence. Sunni extremists view these processions and other Shia rituals as heretical, leading to violent clashes. In the recent years, the Barelvi Sunni community has also been targeted. The Islamic State (also Daesh, formerly the Islamic State of Iraq and al Sham) is one of the latest entrants into Pakistan's landscape of sectarian violence. As per International Crisis Group (ICG), sectarian conflict in Pakistan is the direct consequence of state policies of Islamization and marginalisation of secular democratic forces.[24] Co-option and patronage of religious parties by successive military governments have brought Pakistan to a point where religious extremism threatens to erode the foundations of the state and society.

Ultimately, religion's role in Pakistani society is complex, carrying both the potential to unite and the capacity to divide. Pakistan's society is definitely very religion oriented but unfortunately Islam has not proven to be much of a binding factor as intended. Prioritizing religion over cultural and ethnic aspirations of the people of Pakistan has been the biggest blunder by successive governments which has started manifesting dangerously in Pakistan. The perpetuity of being in denial only complicates the situation, further widening the fissures in society.

Ethnicity: An Incongruent Faultline

Pakistan is home land to multiple ethnicities based on religion, region, language, culture and so on the clashes among these ethnic groups cause internal instability as well as external threats. Pakistan is a multilingual, multiethnic, multicultural, multireligious state in South Asia, home to people divided by race, sectarianism, and differences in language, culture, and ethnicity. Therefore, the issue with the Pakistani federation extends beyond the discussion of inequality within the federating entities. Since Pakistan's founding, ethnicity has posed the biggest threat to its integrity.

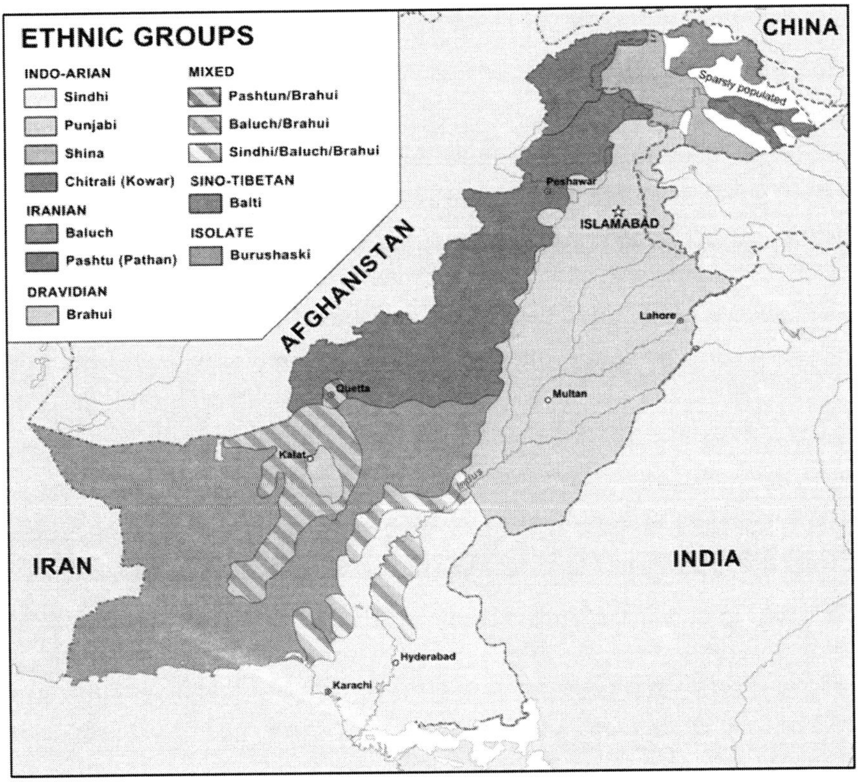

Fig 3.2: Ethnic Groups in Pakistan[25]

There is hardly any state in the world, which is not ethnically plural. Pakistan is also no exception in this regard. Pakistan is a multi-lingual, multi-ethnic, multi-cultural and a multi-religious state, home to people divided by their differences. The ethnic groups in Pakistan includes Punjabis, Pashtuns, Sindhis, Balochs and Muhajirs. Saraikis, Hindkowans/Hazarewals, Brahuis,

Kohistanis, Shina, Baltis, Kashmiris, Paharis, Chitralis and Torwalis are other ethnicities but in smaller numbers. Historical baggage compounded with political prejudice and biased economic policies has led to lasting discontentment and alienation of various ethnic groups, manifesting into separatist movements in few instances. Despite the common religious linkage of Islam, the major ethno-linguistic groups have failed to converge.

The Muslim population in pre-divided India comprised of three communities. The first one was the 'conquerors' who came from the North-West along with their entourage. This group had always enjoyed a sense of superiority and political power. The second group was the immigrants who came to India under the Muslim rule who were mostly Turkish, Pathans, Persian, Arab and Central Asian. They had come to India to seek a better life for themselves. Since they were believed to share a common ethnic background with the conquerors, they were allowed economic and political opportunities and integrated with the ruling elite. The third group comprised of the local converts who were never able to integrate with the Muslim elites. Another reason for them being at the lowest of the social ladder was because they did not share any ethnic lineage with the other better off Muslim communities. This shows how powerful common ethnic origin or lineage was in India and how it divided the Muslims of the subcontinent. Ethnicity was far more powerful in keeping the different Muslim communities separated and divided, much stronger than the aspect of common religion in India.

Today, Pakistan comprises four administrative units (Punjab, Sindh, Khyber Pakhtunkhwa and Baluchistan), one federal territory (the Islamabad Capital Territory) and two occupied territories (Pakistan Occupied Kashmir and Gilgit-Baltistan). The country follows a federal structure, which, in theory, divides power between the centre and the provinces. Official terminology of Pakistan also designates ethnicity as 'provincialism' or 'regionalism'. Each province in Pakistan has its own culture, language and history which instils an ethnocentric pride amongst each ethnic community. However, conflicts between the provinces have dominated Pakistan politics since the country's inception in 1947, with several regions demanding autonomy or independence. The history of the country, the size of the provinces, socio-cultural divisions, power imbalances and the separation of Bangladesh have all resulted in long standing tensions between the different regions. Author Smruti Pattanaik describes Pakistan's quest for federalism in damning terms, noting that "the ruling elites in Pakistan in their quest for nationalism and national unity have always tried to suppress any spirit of genuine federalism perceiving it as a prelude to separatism."[26] However, in their attempt to quash separatism, these elites may have inadvertently catalysed it instead.

Balochs primarily reside in Baluchistan, Pakistan's largest province by area, but significant Baloch populations also exist in other parts of Pakistan, particularly in Sindh and Punjab. The current situation in Baluchistan is rooted in the complex history of the erstwhile state of Kalat which became a British protectorate, but never, as Baloch nationalists proudly note, an Indian princely state. After the British left, Kalat was forced to accede to Pakistan. Facing neglect and disdain from the successive governments in Pakistan alienated the region which transformed into an armed struggle by Balochs for their rightful place in the country. Today we are witnessing the fifth 'insurgency' in Baluchistan, after 1948, 1958, 1962 and 1973–77 marked by unprecedented violence, sectarian terrorism, enforced disappearances and rampant human rights violations.

Despite being rich in natural gas, coal, copper and gold, most of Baluchistan's population remains impoverish with lack of access to primary education, healthcare and basic infrastructure. Exploitation of these resources has been a major source of discontent. As Islamabad reaps economic benefit, people of Baluchistan continue to live in poverty. As per Federal budget of Pakistan 2024-25, Baluchistan was provided PKR 667.55 Billion in comparison to PKR 3.69 Trillion allotted to Punjab (amounting to almost five time the budget).[27] The region has gained economic and strategic importance, especially after construction of CPEC linking Western China with Gwadar. This geo-strategic context has added further complexity to the Baluchistan conundrum. The Balochs fear that instead of bringing prosperity to the region, CPEC would inflict discrimination, deflect development, bring in unwelcomed immigration and cause a heavy drain on its natural resources. The policy of Pakistan government of resource extraction without compensation or rare investment is an example of economic colonialism that has resulted in ethnic Balochs to feel alienated.

Complex relationship between the Pakistani state and Baluchistan is often marked by mistrust and resentment. Islamabad has largely focused on control rather than integration, a stance that has left Baluchistan in perpetual marginalisation. Tilak Devasher opines that Pakistan's perpetual failure to address the region's core issues which are economic deprivation, lack of political representation and cultural autonomy has kept the fire of rebellion alive for many decades. The recent attacks by Baluchistan Liberation Army (BLA) and other splinter armed groups against the Punjabis and in few instances even the Chinese nationals working on CPEC, reflects the sense of belligerence and hatred that has developed against the non-natives and foreigners.

Pakistan's iron fist approach in handling Baluchistan has not delivered much. Since inception of Pakistan, the government has treated the Baloch independence movement as a national security issue rather than a political or economic one. The road to peace and integration in Baluchistan lies not in military domination, but in addressing the legitimate demands of the Baloch people in terms of economic inclusion, political representation and respect for cultural identity. Mass movements lead by the likes of Mahrang Baloch, a young charismatic woman leader, reflects the latest wave of Baloch Nationalism which has shaken up the edifice of Pakistan's federal structure in the country. Until Baluchistan is handled with dexterity, it is likely to remain an Achilles heel in the rapidly deteriorating security situation in the region.

The Pashtuns are an ethnic group that mainly reside in parts of North-West Pakistan, and South-East Afghanistan, dispersed from Indus to Hindu Kush. Provisional results from the census conducted in 2017 indicated that there are more than 33 Million Pashtuns in Pakistan.[28] The figure of 33 Million has been disputed by Pashtun leaders who feel that it under-represents the community casting aspersions on the process of enumeration itself as an official tool to entrench the domination of Punjab over other states. In the last two centuries, this region has been invaded by each of the great powers of the times; Great Britain in the 19th Century, when the Pashtuns became pawns in the chessboard of the Great Game between Great Britain and Russia; the Soviet Union in the 20th Century when they became victims of the Cold War between the United States and the USSR, and were subjected to an invasion and a destructive civil war; and the United States in the 21st Century when the Pashtuns became a central factor in the GWOT and its aftermath.

Durand Line is the biggest bone of contention impacting Pashtun identity. The demarcation was negotiated in 1893 between the colonial diplomat, Henry Mortimer Durand (1850-1924), and the Afghan Amir (ruler) Abdul Rahman (1844-1901).[29] The primary aim of the line was to delineate the spheres of influence of the British in India and the Afghan Amir. Pakistan inherited the boundary when it emerged as an independent country in 1947. Afghanistan does not, however, recognise the legitimacy of this border. Today, the Pashtuns of both Pakistan and Afghanistan are emotional in opposing the Durand Line both ideologically as well as politically. This transnational sense of identity has contributed to the idea of a unified Pashtun homeland or a state of Pashtunistan, even if political aspirations for such a state have been less prominent in recent years. Pashtun tribes are widely said to be held together by their adherence to a shared culture and commitment to a tribal code called 'Pastunwali'. Pashtunwali, is founded on the principles on nang (honour), melmatsya (hospitality) and badal (reciprocity), laying stress on the need for decisions to be made by thc Jirga (or tribal council). Pashtunwali with Pashto being the primary language, determines the behaviour of the Pashtuns in many ways.

The Pashtun community in Pakistan face a complex set of challenges, ranging from political marginalization, social discrimination and economic hardship amidst serious security concerns. Colonial ethnographic assumptions of the tribal nature of the Pashtuns, coupled with their strategic interests of developing a buffer between India and Afghanistan, led to these tribal areas being regulated by a distinct legal and political framework – one that was apparently more akin to the governance of tribal societies. The Frontier Crimes Regulation (FCR), enacted in 1901 by the British colonial government, was a special legal framework designed to administer the tribal areas. This model of governance was essentially maintained by Pakistan until 2018 when the areas of the FATA were formally incorporated into Khyber Pakhtunkhwa as part of 25th Constitutional Amendment which abolished the FCR and extended the jurisdiction of the Supreme Court and Peshawar High Court to the former tribal areas.[30] However, this transition has been challenging. The lack of proper infrastructure, representation and legal integration of FATA into the national framework has led to staggered development in these areas furthering greater social alienation.

Pashtun Tahafuz Movement (PTM) is a campaign that advocates justice for Pashtuns in response to the violence and military repression in Pashtun dominated areas. The PTM has frequently condemned the abuses committed by both militants and the state, including extrajudicial killings and enforced disappearances of Pashtuns. The Pakistani establishment accuses the PTM of being a proxy of Afghanistan and India, propped up to destabilise Pakistan. Major General Asif Ghafoor, former DG ISPR (Inter Services Public Relations) echoed this official narrative when he described the PTM as a movement that was being manipulated by the 'enemies of Pakistan'. The establishment also presents the PTM as a movement that poses a law and order problem, and accuses it of fermenting violence against the state. A number of Pashtuns partaking in PTM protests have been arrested under charges of sedition and terrorism. The bitterness of Pashtuns is clearly reflected in the fact that a popular slogan used by the PTM and its supporters is *'ye jo deshat gardi hai, is ke peeche vardi hai'* (the uniform is behind this terrorism). This slogan is, of course, a play on a popular song celebrating the contributions of the Pakistani military to the state, *'ye jo jurat mandi hai, is ke peeche vardi hai'* (the uniform is the cause of this courage).

In the recent years, relationship between the Pashtuns and the Tehrik-e-Taliban Pakistan (TTP) has evolved significantly, shaped by both ethnic and political dynamics. Many of the TTP's foot soldiers and leaders are Pashtuns. The group's initial base of support was in Pashtun-majority regions, particularly in FATA and KPK. Operation Zarb-e-Azb (2014–2017), a major military operation targeting militant groups, particularly in North Waziristan, resulted in significant civilian casualties and displacement. An estimated One million people were displaced due to military operations in these areas.[31] Thousands were injured or killed as a result of both the operations and the subsequent terrorist retaliation. TTP has often exploited local Pashtun grievances, particularly those arising from the Pakistani government's military operations. TTP has framed itself as a defender of Pashtun rights, positioning itself as resisting both the Pakistani government and foreign influence. While the TTP found some support among certain Pashtun segments, many Pashtuns also oppose the TTP's violent tactics and its attempts to impose its extremist ideology.

Issues of Pashtun identity, autonomy, human rights violation and justice remain central to the Pashtun discourse in both Afghanistan and Pakistan. Resurgence of TTP and other terrorist groups post-2021 and the resultant military scramble by Pakistan has once again brought forth the issue of Pashtun nationalism. Islamabad's Pashtunistan puzzle is not new, but given the vicious potential of terrorism in the region, the stakes for resolving the puzzle are much higher. Afghan Taliban's disdainful refusal to treat Khyber Pakhtunkhwa as Pakistani province is tantamount to calling for Pashtun unity which exacerbates Pakistan's problems with the Pashtuns manifold.

Gilgit-Baltistan, previously known as the Northern Areas, is part of Jammu and Kashmir and under illegal occupation of Pakistan. Gilgit-Baltistan covers approx. 72,971 Square Kilometers with an estimated population of 1.2 million which includes four denominations of Islam viz. Shias (39%), Sunnis (27%), Ismailis (18%), and Noorbakshis (16%) besides at least 24 other ethnic and linguistic groups. Shina, Balti, Khowar (Chitrali), Wakhi and Nuristanis are the major ethnicities in the region.[32] There are also Pashtuns in the area, especially in the Diamer district, who speak Pashto and follow Sunni Islam. The primary ethnic problem in Gilgit-Baltistan is a deep-rooted sectarian divide between the majority Sunni Muslim population and the Shia Muslim minority, which has deep historical roots. This often leads to tensions and violence, particularly aggravated by political and religious influences from outside the region including those from neighbouring countries such as Iran and Saudi Arabia, which have sought to influence the religious dynamics of the region. The historical divide has resulted in feelings of marginalization among the Shia community and occasional outbreaks of sectarian violence.

While Shina speakers are the majority in the Gilgit District, other ethnic groups, such as the Balti and Khowar, feel side-lined politically. The Balti people, especially in Baltistan, have often expressed dissatisfaction with the lack of political representation in the provincial and national governments. There is an ongoing demand for greater political autonomy and representation for the people of Gilgit-Baltistan. The Balti and the Khowar speakers in Chitral, have expressed concerns over being overshadowed by the Shina-speaking Gilgit region. Some groups argue that the Gilgit district receives more attention and resources, leaving other regions like Baltistan underdeveloped. Some communities in Gilgit-Baltistan, particularly the Balti and Wakhi, have strong cultural ties to Tibetan and Central Asian heritage, which sometimes leads to clashes with the dominant South Asian cultural narrative. These groups feel their unique identities and histories are not being preserved or recognized by the central government.

The history of violence in Gilgit-Baltistan has been marked by frequent clashes between the Shia and the Sunnis. The most significant outbreak occurred in 1988 following a dispute over moon sighting during Ramadan, leading to large-scale riots and hundreds of deaths; further incidents of violence have been triggered by controversies surrounding religious education and the introduction of Sunni-centric curriculum in schools, often aggravated by the Pakistani government's perceived support of the Sunni minority. The Karakoram Highway, which connects Pakistan to China, has also played a noticeable role in the sectarian conflict. This strategic highway has brought economic opportunities and development to the region but has also exposed Gilgit-Baltistan to external influences of sectarian ideologies.

The people of Gilgit-Baltistan have long demanded full provincial status, as the region remains governed by the Gilgit-Baltistan Empowerment and Self-Governance Order of 2009, which does not grant the region the same rights as Pakistan's provinces.[33] This lack of political power has caused frustration among local ethnic groups, who feel sidelined in national decision-making processes. Muffled voices in support or re-integration with India are also not uncommon. Overall, a marked neglect, disregard for the cultural identity of the tribes and rising stakes of China in the region have fuelled separatist aspirations in the tribes of Gilgit-Baltistan.

Sindhudesh (literally 'land for the Sindhis') is an idea for a separate homeland for the Sindhi nationalists in Pakistan. The demand for Sindhudesh has varied over time, ranging from demanding more political, economic and social rights to outright separation from the federation of Pakistan. The movement was historically conceived by the Sindhi political leader G.M. Syed in opposition to the One Unit policy, the imposition of Urdu by the central government and presence of a large number of Muhajirs (Indian Muslim refugees) settled in the province. Apart from Syed, the other two most influential leaders shaping the Sindhi nationalist cause included Ibrahim Joyo and Shaikh Ayaz, jointly referred to as the 'Sufi saints of Sindhi nationalism'. Syed, endured nearly 30 years of incarceration for Sindhi nationalist politics. He gave an organizational shape to the movement by establishing *Jeay Sindh Mahaz (JSM)* in 1972, which riled the Pakistani state with its open calls for the liberation of Sindh and the establishment of Sindudesh. Given the high-handed approach of the Pakistani Army, the movement gradually descended into an armed struggle where several outfits have taken up the cause of Sindhudesh. Some of the prominent resistance groups include the *Sindhudesh Liberation Army, Jeay Sindh Qaumi Mahaz, Jeay Sindh Muttahida Mahaz and Jeay Sindh Students' Federation* among others.

Over the years, thousands of Sindhis, political workers and human rights activists have disappeared. The Government of Pakistan in 2021 asserted that it gave closure to nearly 5000 cases of enforced disappearances, even as over 2000 remain unresolved.[34] However, these claims have been disputed by the rights groups, accusing the government of deflating the actual numbers. A September 2023 report by the Human Rights Commission of Pakistan denounced the Pakistani government over the human rights situation in Northern Sindh, including violations of rights, precarious law and order, poor access to education and healthcare and other restrictions on fundamental freedom.[35] The concept of Sindhudesh is also supported by the Sindhi diaspora including Sindhis in India, most of whom had to be relocated out of Sindh after Partition, leaving behind their property as evacuee trusts under reciprocal government supervision.

Today, once again the idea of Sindh nationalism has taken the centre stage. According to World Sindhi Congress Chairman Lakhu Luhana, the current resurgence is a result of resentment of the Sindhi people against what they see as systematic demographic re-engineering, by promoting large scale migration of Punjabis to Sindh.[36] What is dreaded that colonial treatment of Sindh by Pakistan will culminate in a situation similar to Bangladesh which broke away from Pakistan under duress of ethnic and linguistic marginalization.

Punjab is the largest province in Pakistan in terms of population and enjoys a vital position in politics. The dominant role of Punjab has been under criticism in the political history in the past but now it has taken a serious mood. The protagonists of this division claim that this province is multilingual and it should be divided on ethnic lines. Even elites from other provinces favor the division to eliminate the powerful position of Punjab but division of Punjab within the given political framework will make the ethnic plurality in Pakistan more problematic and leave an enduring impact on other provinces.

Punjab is the largest province in Pakistan in terms of population and enjoys a vital position in politics. Saraiki ethno-linguistic movement is one of the recent developments in national politics, though its origins can be traced back in the early history of Pakistan. The core demand of this movement is the establishment of South Punjab or a Saraiki province or Saraikistan as the fifth province of Pakistan to include the three divisions of Punjab i.e., Bahawalpur, Dera Ghazi Khan and Multan. Some Saraiki ethno-nationalists also call for inclusion of adjoining districts of Khyber Pakhtunkhwa, Baluchistan and Sindh. Even the elites from other provinces favour the division to dilute the unbridled power concentrated in Punjab. There are many reasons for the emergence of Saraiki movement of which economic isolation and social repudiation are the biggest factors. Saraiki people are aggrieved by the suppression of their culture and linguistic identity by the Punjabi Muhajir establishment and political elite. Saraiki was not accorded the status of a separate language till as late as 1981. It is essential to keep in mind that Saraiki identity is not a pure ethnic identity based upon actual or imagined blood-ties or common ancestry. There are many Baloch and Pashtun tribes living in the Saraiki belt and speak Saraiki language. Saraiki is mainly a linguistic identity, though the prospects of becoming an ethnic identity in future cannot be ignored. Southern Punjab is a region which has maximum number of madrassas and mosques, often referred to as a 'nursery of radicalism'. Most of the terrorist tanzeems have their recruitment wings in this region which are flourishing with impunity. Strangely, this is also the area from where maximum recruits into Army are drawn besides a large number of officers. Complexity of this region in terms of political, social, linguistic and religious sensitivity renders South Punjab or the 'Saraiki Belt' most sensitive from a security perspective.

In the overall context, the inability of the state to homogenize all ethnicities with a common thread of nationalism and brazen domination by the Punjabis in every field has led to mass inequality in the society. Pakistan has tried to take the 'nation-state' approach for crafting a unifying identity for itself which has proven to be catastrophic. Repeated failure of Pakistan in bringing together various ethnicities under a common umbrella has emerged as a critical faultline in Pakistan which threatens to shred the very idea of Pakistan into tatters.

Military: The Consequential Fault Line

Georg Henirich von Berenhorst, a Prussian military writer had said, "Prussia always remained not a country with an army, but an army with a country".[37] This simile has often been used for Pakistan given the power and influence wielded by the Army in the affairs of the state. Pakistan is deemed 'authoritarian' due to the pervasive influence of and interventions by its powerful Army, which shapes and often controls the nation's political dynamics. The elections in February 2024 adequately demonstrates Pakistan Army's influence in domestic political process. The outcome of the polls indicates a sophisticated electioneering, with military shaping the face of the government. Today both Imran Khan and Nawaz Sharif have been effectively side-lined, affianced into legal complications. But is this power of Army absolute? Violent protests by PTI supporters on 09 May 2023 after the arrest of Imran Khan targeting military installations including the residence of Corps Commander at Lahore was an unprecedented escalation not seen earlier in the history of Pakistan. Amidst deteriorating economic situation, Pakistan Army's big spendings are being questioned. The internal security situation has been in turmoil. Pakistan Army has repeatedly suffered casualties both in Khyber Pakhtunkhwa and Baluchistan facing criticism for its inept handling of the situation. The radical terrorist groups and organizations which were nursed as strategic assets are turning around to bite the hand that fed them. Pakistan Army as an institute is obviously under stress but definitely not vanquished. It therefore merits to analyse the characteristics of Pakistan Army as an institution which lends strength to the state while at the same time also making it more vulnerable.

In Pakistan, Army and politics is synonymous. There are several reasons that makes Pakistan Army the institution that it has come to being. However, the most significant factor has been the existence of an extremely weak and crippled polity which has repeatedly failed to provide the much-needed leadership to the country. After partition of India, Pakistan had aspired to develop democratic institutions like any new nation but failed to do so miserably. Pakistan could not put together a constitution for almost nine years within which it changed its Prime Minister for seven times. According to

Philip Oldenburg (2010), Jinnah as the first Governor General, concentrated all executive, legislative and political positions in himself, reducing the powers of prime minister significantly while increasing the authority of bureaucracy and military.[38] After the death of Jinnah and assassination of Liaquat Ali Khan in 1951, Governor General Ghulam Muhammad came to power and dismissed the Constituent Assembly, which strengthened the alliance between the military and bureaucracy and reinforced military supremacy. A society that lacks effective political culture will leave the military establishments or institutions as the only body to govern.

Pakistan's history is replete with instances of direct or indirect military interference in domestic politics, including four periods of martial law. However, today there is a growing discontent with military's interference in politics. This sentiment was evident in the 2024 General elections, where voters expressed frustration by supporting candidates opposing military-backed figures, signalling a potential shift in public perception. The brazenness with which electoral manipulation took place during the elections has caused widespread anger among people against the Army's leadership. Allegations of rigging notwithstanding, the military appears to have achieved its intended objectives without caring much about the people's mandate. Irrespective of these feeble signatures of public resistance to military's dominance in political sphere, the institution continues to maintain substantial control.

Another important facet of Pakistan Army is the relationship it has fostered with Islamist organizations nurtured as a strategic asset to dominate the national politics and to keep India unsettled. In order to achieve these objectives, the military has to give these organisations and their affiliates (like the Sunni terrorist outfits of Lashkar-e-Jhangvi, Lashkar-e-Tayyeba/Jamaat-ud-Dawa (LeT/JuD), Jaish-e-Muhammed (JeM) etc.) more space to operate. This means that any clean-up operation which is launched against rogue or recalcitrant jihadist groups is by definition selective and must leave the 'good' jihadists untouched. This is precisely what has created the existential challenge that Pakistan confronts today. In the domestic sphere, the military needs the support of fringe religious parties and groups to keep the civilian government under pressure. The military's backing has strengthened these parties far beyond their popular support and has bestowed upon them a virtual veto over the direction that the polity and society take. These parties stand as a bulwark against any progressive or liberal legislation, which, in turn, has opened the field for extremism and intolerance to sweep through the society. The result is substantial support and sympathy for the radical Islamist groups which are taking on the Pakistani authorities both militarily and ideologically.

Islamization of Pakistan Army is a boiling pot. Despite obvious religious connotations, the founding fathers of Pakistan did not want the Army to be overly influenced by religious dogma. Instead, they wanted to preserve the Sandhurst traditions in the Army in the initial phases and later adopted the West Point pattern, ethos and practices. Senior Generals like Ayub Khan not only behaved like the erstwhile British officers, they wanted others also to follow suit.[39] There was a conscious effort not to allow a greater role for religion in the Army than what had been the British practice. Religion was used to bind fresh recruits to their units through oaths and to indoctrinate them in virtuosity and religion. However, this use of religion was never encouraged to go overboard. Overall Pakistan Army remained insular to religious influence and maintained an imperial character borrowed from a British legacy.

The creeping process of Islamization became an open and mass movement after Zia-ul-Haq's advent on the national political scene. His policies not only shaped the Army's internal culture but also influenced regional geo-politics and civil-military relations in Pakistan for decades. Many have argued that Zia's Islamization drive was perhaps as much inspired by his personal religious convictions, as by the political compulsion at that time. It was loudly proclaimed that Pakistan was being converted into a pure Islamic nation in accordance with the ethos of the Pakistan Movement with Army being the 'guardians of its ideological frontiers'. The first visible impact of the creeping Islamic ethos was in the Officers' Messes where public consumption of alcohol began to be frowned upon. The mass compulsory prayers in a Unit on Fridays, a practice inherited from the British era, acquired more importance and became almost compelling events.

The heraldic slogan of Pakistan Army from Jinnah's days – "Unity, Faith and Discipline" was changed to "Iman, Taqwa, Jihad fi Sabeelillah" (Faith, Obedience of God and Struggle for the path of Allah).[40] For the first time the Army began to recruit madrassa products as officers and soldiers. Visit by Tablighi Jamaats to Army Units was allowed. Observance of religious practices and beliefs became an important part of Annual Confidential Reports of the rank and file and became a major determining factor in career progression. The Islamic training and thought were also introduced as part of the training courses at various regimental and training centres in addition to the western oriented training courses and programmes. The attempt was to create an Army with western operating procedures but with an Islamic mind and heart.

The best example of the impact of new Islamic concepts of warfare on the prevailing Pakistani military doctrine and strategies comes from the book 'Quranic Concepts of War' by Brig. (then serving) S.K. Malik.[41] The significance of this book and its theories should be obvious from the fact that it had a foreword by General Zia-ul Haq and a preface by Zia's chief legal adviser A.K. Brohi. According to Malik, Islam divided the world into two camps – the Dar-ul Islam (the world of Islam in which the people had submitted to Allah and his commandments) and the Dar-ul Harb (in which people were still defiant of Allah and the Quran). As a result, repeated conflicts between the believers and the non-believers became inevitable, until the latter were made subservient to Allah. A.K. Brohi, in his preface, stated that the book made it clear that the non-believer – the 'cancerous malformation' – must be removed from the world through 'surgical means', if necessary.

The integration of 'terror' into military concepts of war and strategy and involvement of civilians in a so-called holy war naturally led to evolution of the idea of non-state actors. The launching of various civilian militant groups during Zia-ul-Haq's time could be traced to the evolution of this military doctrine. SSP and its militant wing the Lashkar-e-Jhangvi were floated to quell Shiite and Christian opposition to pro-Sunni Islamization measures and the promulgation of Blasphemy Law, respectively. Pretty soon this doctrine of 'terror' was married to 1976 White Paper on Kashmir brought out by Zulfiqar Ali Bhutto regime and Kashmir specific terror groups were launched, beginning with JKLF and then Jammat-e-Islami floated Hizb-ul Mujahideen besides others.[42]

In the subsequent period there was a clampdown in Islamic ardour especially in regulating life in the Army Garrisons. However, Islamization of Pakistan Army has left the institution permanently plagued with element of religious fanaticism. In July 2007, Pakistan Army launched an operation against Lal Masjid in Islamabad, wherein radical clerics and armed militants were advocating Sharia law. The military siege led to violent clashes and death of over 100 terrorists. Many Army personnel including officers had sympathized with the Lal Masjid cause, leading to internal discontent. In May 2011, Brigadier Ali Khan, a senior officer, was arrested for plotting against the government and having ties with Hizb-ut-Tahrir – an international Islamist group advocating the establishment of an Islamic caliphate.[43] Investigations revealed that Khan had been in contact with Hizb ut-Tahrir and sought to influence fellow officers to rebel against the Army. In 2011, Mumtaz Qadri, a member of Punjab Police's elite force, assassinated Salman Taseer, the Governor of Punjab, over his opposition to blasphemy laws. While Qadri was convicted and executed in 2016, his actions triggered public rallies where some serving and retired military personnel expressed support for his cause. The attack on Pakistan's Naval Base PNS Mehran at Karachi in 2011 resulted in destruction of several US supplied aircrafts. It was later discovered that sympathizers within the Pakistan Navy had aided the terrorists in the attack. In 2012, Major Khalid Mehmood and four other officers were arrested for planning to overthrow the government. These incidents highlight a persistent undercurrent of religious fanaticism within sections of Pakistan Army. Historic policies of fostering Islamist militants for strategic objectives continue to create ideological fractures within Army which is a potential threat to Pakistan's internal security and regional stability.

Pakistan Army's Milbus has been under scrutiny. Over the decades, Pakistan Army has extracted a lion's share in the national budget (over 70%, as per an informal estimate) both directly and indirectly. This allocation isn't just to pay for the defence of Pakistan, but for keeping up the trappings of luxury in their 'deep state'. The armed forces are Pakistan's largest land holders (43% of the country's land is in their control) and they have multiple agencies that are paid from these funds to run businesses ranging from hospitals to industries. And none of this is audited. Pakistan's military today runs a huge commercial empire. Although it is not possible to give a definitive value of the military's internal economy because of the lack of transparency, the estimated worth runs into billions of dollars. Moreover, the military's two business groups – the Fauji Foundation and the Army Welfare Trust – are the largest business conglomerates in the country. Besides these, there are multiple channels through which the military acquires opportunities to monopolize national resources.

In her book 'Military Inc. – Inside Pakistan's Military Economy', Pakistani author Ayesha Siddiqa has put forward three arguments to substantiate Pakistan Army's economic aspirations.[44] **Firstly**, Milbus is military capital that perpetuates Pakistan Army's political predatory style. The defining feature of such predatory capital is that it is concealed, not recorded as part of the defence budget and entails unexplained and questionable transfer of resources from the public to the private sector, especially to individuals or groups of people connected with the armed forces. **Secondly**, Army's economic adventures strengthen its totalitarian system. Motivated by personal gain, the officer cadre of the armed forces seek political and economic relationships which will enable them to increase their economic returns. Milbus is part of the tribute that the Army extracts for providing services such as national security. **Thirdly**, the military's economic predatoriness, especially inside its national boundaries, is both a cause and effect of a feudal authoritarian, and non-democratic political system. In a similar way to other ruling elites such as the feudal landowners and large entrepreneurs, the Army also exploits resources for the advantage of its personnel as part of the pre-capitalist politico-economic system.

While Pakistan Army is seen as a stabilizing force by some, its interventions in civilian affairs and strategic policies have created deep divisions that today threatens nation's unity, democracy and long-term stability. Its overreach in politics, economics and society undermines democratic governance, fosters violence and alienates provincial parties. Pakistan Army's dominance will continue to pose structural challenges to Pakistan's unity, stability and development.

Economy: The Consistent Fault line

Pakistan is grappling with one of its most severe economic crises, characterized by soaring inflation and a depreciating currency. Despite its strategic location and a youthful population, the nation has been trapped in a cycle of economic instability, marked by excessive national debt and reliance on foreign aid. The roots of Pakistan's economic woes trace back to its inception in 1947, where it inherited a limited industrial base and faced political instability. Experts argue that significant policy missteps, resource misallocation, and a failure to invest in education and human capital have exacerbated the situation. Perpetual political instability, cycling through periods of democracy and military rule has only made things worse. Of the country's 29 Prime Ministers, not a single one has completed their five-year term, all either being dismissed or overthrown.[45] As a result, the economy has also suffered miserably, with the status of being in ICU permanently. Today, Pakistan's economy is plagued with high inflation rates (had touched 38% in 2023), trade deficits and debt. Dropping the cap on Pakistani Rupee, as directed by IMF, has resulted in rapid devaluation of the currency. The pandemic, Russia-Ukraine conflict, yearly floods and political instability, all have contributed in creating the current crisis at hand. But the downfall of economy is not recent. It is an outcome of several years of neglect, lack of financial vision and rampant abuse by power bearers which has cumulatively dragged Pakistan into deep dungeons of fiscal instability. Economic duress has affected the society in a manner that it assumes proportion of a national catastrophe threatening to destabilize the nation.

Pakistan's debt problem started in the 1970s, when the government borrowed to cope with the impact of high oil prices. The response of the state to this debt crisis has been to continuously obtain bailout loans from the IMF. As of September 2024, Pakistan had received 25 loans from the IMF which is one of the most sustained periods of lending to any country. The bailout loans have resulted in the debt being passed down generations, giving the IMF an enormous leverage over Pakistan through the economic conditions the institution has placed upon the country. Inability to repay loans also stems from flawed tax collection regime in the country. According to Professor Tariq Banuri at the University of Utah, "Pakistan is one of the world's worst performers on tax collection with the government allowing exemption of taxes on agricultural income and real estate".[46] The government has also avoided aggressive tax policies out of fear of upsetting powerful businesses and the Army. Among the IMF's biggest debtors, Pakistan has the lowest tax revenue as a percentage of GDP at 10%. The lack of tax revenue ensures that there are not enough funds to modernise state-owned enterprises and improve public goods, or repay loans on time, which has led to increased borrowing and debt. This vicious cycle has only been exacerbated by high inflation and currency depreciation.

Pakistan also imports a lot of its food and fuel, meaning they constantly record trade deficits. With depleted foreign currency reserves (which had dwindled to just about $4 billion in June 2024) there is not enough to support even a month's worth of expenditure. As a consequence, Pakistan has been repeatedly pleading its creditors (to include Saudi Arabia, UAE, China and many more) to roll over their debts which has become a norm rather an exception. The damaging effects of repeated bailouts is at its peak – what economists refer to as 'moral hazard'. Erosion of trust between the people and state institutions has exacerbated an already precarious situation. It does appear that Pakistan has finally hit rock bottom with nowhere to go but up, except that the 'rock' keeps sinking.

Pakistan's energy sector in disarray is another important factor which has affected the economy adversely. The challenge stem from poor governance, inefficiency and external dependencies which has created a cycle of power shortages, rising costs and fiscal burdens. In addition to outage-related inefficiencies, the increased costs for utilities have been pushed onto consumers impacting many poorer consumers who have been hit harder than the rest. Pakistan's energy crisis has resulted in a loss of $82 billion in GDP between 2007 and 2020, and a 23% reduction in per capita GDP. The total economic cost of distortions in the power sector in Pakistan is estimated to be $17.69 billion (about 6.5% of GDP) in FY2015.[47]

The introduction of CPEC was seen as a transformative step for Pakistan's economy, aimed at improving infrastructure and energy production. However, the initiative has resulted in increased debt, with Pakistan owing approximately $26.6 billion to China by 2022. This financial burden raises concerns about long-term sustainability and the economic viability of projects that were expected to stimulate growth. Ensuring the safety of Chinese personnel and project sites remains a crucial challenge, especially in Baluchistan.

Terrorism: The Threatening Fault line

As per South Asia Terrorism Portal, there are 151 major terrorist groups active in Pakistan besides a number of proxies and pseudonyms. Pakistan Army today is experiencing a ternary pull, stretched along the western and eastern borders besides grappling with an extremely sensitive internal security situation. According to figures from the Centre for Research and Security Studies, an Islamabad-based think tank, 2024 was the deadliest year in nearly a decade for Pakistan. The data reveals that 2,526 people were killed in various attacks last year – including nearly 700 security personnel, more than 900 civilians, and approximately 900 armed fighters. Today most of the terrorist organizations and groups which had enjoyed uncontested patronage of the government and the military have turned belligerent. Obviously, the chicken has come back home to roost.

Pakistan succumbed to the attraction of religious extremism much early. Although most of the Islamic religious parties and organizations were not on the same page as Mohammed Ali Jinnah at the time of partition on the demand for a separate Muslim state. But in due course of time successive governments in chair understood the leverage of religion card which could be invoked to justify military and political aspirations. Whether it was in support of successive attempts to seize Kashmir through mobilization of hybrid elements or sanctify controversial strategic decisions, the religious sentiment proved beneficial.

Religious fundamentalism took a major step forward in Pakistan from the mid-1970s, especially after Zia-ul-Haq assumed power in the country. He prepared Pakistani society for a long-proxy war, first in Afghanistan against the Soviet Union and then in Kashmir. Zia called upon the Ulema, or mullahs, to legitimize his unconstitutional rule which changed the very complexion of Pakistani society. Sectarian groups like Sipah-i-Sahaba and Tehrik-i-Jafena surfaced and flourished under Zia's patronage. The regime of General Zia also saw the rise of Islamic militants in the political system. The two main Islamic parties of Pakistan, Jamiat-ulema-i-Islam (JUI) and Jamaat-i-Islamic (JI) became actively involved in Afghanistan, first in the anti-Soviet jihad and later in support of the Taliban. As a fallout from Afghan turmoil, guns, drugs and state sponsored terrorism proliferated a mafia-like culture in parts of Pakistan thereby creating a threat to internal security and stability.

Post Soviet-Afghan war, the mujahedeen were left at the disposal of Pakistan Army which employed them liberally to fuel the Kashmir proxy war. This was a period which witnessed intense counter terrorist operations in Kashmir resulting in huge casualties on both sides. With Global War on Terrorism, Pakistan was caught in a quandary, supporting western forces on one hand while sympathizing with the Taliban on the other side. Much like Zia-ul-Haq, Musharraf had told the world that jihad in its true understanding delineates war cultures and shuns terrorism.[48] The implied meaning of his statement was that his military regime had no control over the mujahedeen, whom he called freedom fighters, and that their actions were purely voluntary. The double speak did no better good to Pakistan and soon the cash cows started running dry. Neutralization of Osama Bin Laden in Abbotabad turned out to be good closure for coalition forces who were getting increasing frustrated with Taliban eventually resulting in complete drawdown in 2020.

There are several types of terrorist groups which have mushroomed in Pakistan and operating with impunity. These groups can be distinguished by their sectarian background (Ahl-e-Hadith, Deobandi, Jamaat-e-Islami etc.), and their areas of operation (Afghanistan, India, Pakistan). Their objectives may vary from overthrowing the Pakistani government, seizure of Kashmir or support the Afghan Taliban but all enjoy intransigent support of the people of Pakistan to varying extent. Pakistan Taliban or Tehrik-e-Taliban Pakistan is a group which has emerged as a major challenge for Pakistan Army. It is an alliance of militant networks formed in 2007 to unify opposition against the Pakistan Army. Ideologically linked to the Taliban in Afghanistan the group has been waging a bloody war against Pakistan Army for many years. Army's inability to rein in the militant group is a classic demonstration of the chaos that has descended upon Pakistan consuming the country and its resources like a parasite.

Overall, the major issue with the existence of Islamic Terrorist Groups in Pakistan is the deeply entrenched influence that they have come to bear on the society both ideologically and materially. The situation has got critically exacerbated with emergence of armed separatist forces that are potent, well equipped and strong enough to challenge the writ of the military and the state. This cumulative culture of gun wielding in the name of religious obligation with the fervour of separatist agenda is one of the most dangerous faultline emerging in Pakistan today. The targeted attacks on Pakistan Army in Baluchistan and KPK are symbolic of the violence that these forces are capable of delivering which has unnerved the establishment to every bit. Military leverage of hybrid elements sought by Pakistan against India as well as strategic depth desired in Afghanistan appear to be shattered today. The very fact that it has become difficult to prognosticate the outcome of the ongoing contest between the armed terrorist or separatist groups and Pakistan Army gives an estimate of the uncertainty that looms large on Pakistan and its Army.

Demography: The Compounding Fault line

With a population exceeding 240 million and a significant proportion of youth, demography plays a crucial role in shaping Pakistan's social, economic and political landscape. As per State Bank of Pakistan figures, 67% population is less than 30 years of age today. Pakistan's youth represents both an opportunity and a challenge. If equipped with the right skills, this workforce can boost economic output and global competitiveness. However, a large number are drifting toward radical ideologies due to a combination of socioeconomic, political, and psychological factors. This shift poses a serious risk to national security, social cohesion, and long-term stability of Pakistan as well as the region.

As per United Nations Population Fund (UNFPA), in 1990 Pakistan and Bangladesh had similar level of male secondary school enrolment, around 30%, but Bangladesh has subsequently seen a considerably better performance, reaching 67% in 2018 compared to 45% in Pakistan. The current gap for females is even wider. Today at least 20 million Pakistani children are out of school, which will result in the skill level of the workforce lagging behind other countries for the foreseeable future, with negative consequences for its competitiveness. In addition, the gap between male and female education levels means a lack of female empowerment both in the home and the workplace. The education system in Pakistan is not producing the skills and abilities required for a highly productive workforce.

Unemployment is a serious socio-economic challenge for Pakistan, affecting millions of people and contributing to poverty, social unrest, and underdevelopment. With a rapidly growing population and an increasing youth bulge, the country faces a widening gap between job creation and labour market entrants. Unemployment rate in Pakistan is estimated to be around 8-10%, though some analysts believe the actual figure is much higher due to informal labour. The economy cannot provide enough jobs to a number of unemployed youths whereas more and more youths enter the labour force every year. This problem gets compounded with the fact that the education system does not prepare most of its graduates very well for the jobs that exist. The increased level of unemployment increases poverty levels and lowers consumer expenditure. Unhappy individuals turn to either crime or radicalism as they seek alternative ways to deal with their situation.

Pakistan's public education system is underfunded and inaccessible in many areas. Madrassas provide free education, lodging, and meals – an attractive option for low-income families. As of 2023, there were approximately 35,000 registered madrassas across Pakistan although thousands of unregistered institutions also operate informally.[49] Over 3.5 million students are enrolled in madrassas, representing 8-10% of the school-going population. Many parents believe madrassas provide moral upbringing in line with Islamic values. This reinforces the social acceptability of sending children to madrassas. Certain madrassas promote a strict interpretation of Islam that fosters intolerance toward other sects and religions. These madrassas use religious rhetoric to justify violent jihad and glorify martyrdom. Extremist groups often use madrassas to recruit young minds by portraying armed struggle as a religious duty. Various political and religious groups use madrassas to build influence and promote their ideology.

While Pakistan has a large and youthful population, structural challenges are limiting its potential. Without significant investment in education, healthcare, and job creation, the demographic dividend could turn into a demographic burden – leading to rising unemployment, social unrest, inequality and increased poverty which in turn creates a sense of frustration and desperation, making young people vulnerable to extremist narratives that offer a sense of purpose and belonging. A history of conflict, perceived injustice and a lack effective governance has fuelled resentment and alienation amongst the youth, pushing them towards extremist religious groups. Internet and social media platforms play a vital role in spreading extremist propaganda, recruiting members and radicalizing young people. Terrorism and instability besides have significant economic costs has deepened social divides creating an environment of fear and distrust, undermining social cohesion.

Urban-Rural Divide: The Societal Fault Line

The 2017 census in Pakistan reveals that with about 210 million population, Pakistan will leap forward to be the fourth most populous nation in the world by 2030. The census also revealed that the urban population account for about 37%, which increased from 33% as in the 1998 census. The balance population still resides in the rural areas of Pakistan. The feudal system in rural Pakistan directly impacts the social, political, and economic development in rural areas.

Feudalistic structures remain deeply entrenched in Pakistan. The elite class of landlords control vast areas of agricultural land while a majority of rural population work as tenant farmers or landless labourers. Although land reforms were introduced in the 1950s and 1970s, they were either poorly implemented or reversed due to the influence of the feudal elite. Many rural labourers fall into debt bondage, and are still forced to work to repay loans. This practice is especially prevalent in Sindh and Punjab. Although bonded labour is illegal, enforcement is weak due to the power of feudal lords. Feudal families dominate local and national politics.

Many feudal lords hold influential positions in the National Assembly, Senate and provincial assemblies wherein political power is often passed down through family dynasties, limiting democratic participation. Women's right to education, property and social mobility are severely restricted in rural areas. Practices like honour killings, forced child marriages and prosecution of women from minority communities are rampant. Feudal lords have repeatedly resisted land redistribution and taxation on agricultural income, depriving the state of valuable revenue. Overall, the status of rural areas in Pakistan has remained antiquated stuck in the time clock of imperial era. This not only accentuates societal imbalance but in combination with poor governance and unemployment creates conditions for riots, protests and social insurrection.

Urban areas in Pakistan have a unique characteristic. Being centres of trade, industry and governance the impact of economic uncertainty and political fragility is more pronounced in these areas. Areas like Karachi and Lahore, receive disproportionate resources, leaving rural regions in poverty. Pakistan's urban population is growing at around 3% annually, one of the fastest urbanization rates in South Asia. This is primarily due to rural-to-urban migration and natural population growth. Around 40% of urban dwellers live in slums with inadequate access to basic services. Urban transport systems are insufficient, and most cities lack mass transit options except for projects like the Lahore Metro and Karachi's BRT. Urban areas have extreme wealth inequalities, with luxury housing and gated communities including cantonments next to poverty-stricken informal settlements.

The rural-urban divide in Pakistan poses a significant threat to country's stability. Out of the total 40 million living below the poverty line, 30 million live in rural areas. Deteriorating law and order situation in Pakistan along with ongoing economic crisis has made the rural areas feel even more marginalized pushing the gullible youth into the clutches of radical extremist elements. Most of the terrorist tanzeems and organizations draw their cadres from rural areas who can closely relate to the inequalities in the society. This growing disparity between rural and urban area has created an environment of economic inequality, social tension and political unrest, which can undermine national cohesion.

Natural Disasters: Force Majeure Fault Line

Pakistan faces significant challenges from natural disasters like floods, earthquakes, droughts and extreme weather, leading to loss of life, displacement and economic disruption often exacerbated by insufficient preparedness and coordination. Pakistan has one of the highest disaster risk levels in the world, ranked 18 out of 191 countries by the 2019 Inform Risk Index.[50] Natural disasters in Pakistan often displace communities and strain the country's meagre resources. The situation gets further exacerbated due to government's inability to check corruption, poor management, lack of essential infrastructure, inadequate disaster preparedness, political prioritization, deforestation, land degradation and lackadaisical implementation of climate policy.

Over the last few decades, 124 out of 166 districts of Pakistan have experienced a natural disaster of some kind, which has impacted a population of more than 33 million. The country's lowlands which are an integral part of the Indus River system is highly flood-prone. Pakistan has witnessed 29 floods since its independence with a critical flood like disaster situation occurring every year since 2010. Flooding has caused hindrance not only to social growth but also to economic progress in the past few years. In 2022, a third of the nation was submerged by massive and deadly floods across the country. It took 1739 lives causing a loss of $14.9 billion in damage and $15.2 billion in economic terms as per government's damage assessment report. The recurrent floods indicate that the community, local government and related institutions are not sufficiently prepared or equipped to handle the situation which can implode into a national contingency.

Pakistan, located on the boundary of the Indian and Eurasian tectonic plates, is also highly susceptible to earthquakes, with the 2005 Kashmir earthquake being the most destructive, causing over 73,000 deaths and leaving 3.5 million homeless. After almost a decade, another strong earthquake affected the Af-Pak region in 2015. It originated in the mountainous regions of the Hindu Kush. Only in Pakistan, it claimed over 300 lives and injured thousands. Some of the major cities which are thickly populated are located in these zones like Islamabad, Karachi, Quetta, Peshawar, Gawadar, Pasni, Ziarat, and Kalat which are under constant threat from future destruction. Long-term disaster preparedness and mitigation efforts based on improved seismic hazard assessment, micro-zonation, earthquake resistant construction, etc. is missing. In addition to earthquakes, the southern region of Sindh and Baluchistan, experiences frequent droughts due to arid and semi-arid conditions, with the frequency and intensity increasing every year due to climate change. Pakistan's 960 km long coastal belt is also vulnerable to cyclones, causing widespread damage to property with potential loss of life, especially in coastal districts like Gawadar, Badin, and Thatta.

The impact of such disasters extends beyond human and economic losses, affecting political stability, governance, and public trust. Natural disasters destroy critical infrastructure (roads, hospitals, schools), requiring massive public spending for repairs and reconstruction. Increased expenditures for relief efforts may strain national budgets, reduce public services, and create long-term debt. Disasters disrupt industries, agriculture, and trade, leading to economic recession and unemployment. The 2010 floods in Pakistan caused losses of approximately $43 billion, straining public resources and delaying development programs. Disasters can weaken state control in affected areas, allowing extremist groups to exploit the situation. In post-flood Pakistan, extremist groups offered aid in areas where the state was absent, gaining influence and public support.

Natural disasters are not just humanitarian crises – they also present significant challenges to political and economic stability. Some of the more immediate outcome of disasters is felt in the form of displacement, rise in illiteracy, unemployment, health crises, water and food scarcity, infrastructure damages, loss of human lives, destruction of crops, livestock losses, water-borne diseases, outward migration to cities and loss of social capital. The very fact that Pakistan lies along a precarious geography vulnerable to natural disasters necessitates a robust mechanism to respond to such critical situations.

However, the same is not existent nor there has been any sincere effort to develop one which has assumed the proportion of a critical faultline threatening the stability of the state.

Conclusion

Pakistan is currently facing multiple challenges that threaten its stability. Baluchistan has seen a surge in insurgent activities. BLA hijacked a passenger train on 11 Mar 2025, reportedly resulting in the deaths of 21 passengers.[51] BLA has intensified its operations in the recent period, targeting security forces, civilians and infrastructure projects, particularly those involving Chinese investments. In addition, TTP has escalated attacks after ending a ceasefire in late 2022. Pakistan's economy is under pressure, with the central bank recently pausing its series of rate cuts, leaving the interest rate at 12%. This decision reflects concerns over currency stability and a widening trade deficit. The political landscape remains turbulent, with ongoing tensions between PTI and the military establishment. Former Prime Minister Imran Khan's allegations against the military have deepened societal divisions. Pakistan's energy crisis does not seem to go away while it still appears unprepared for anticipated natural disasters especially monsoon floods. Today, Pakistan stares at a future which is uncertain and chaotic. The fault lines that have been discussed in this section are bulging to implode but yet Pakistan holds itself together with a fine tender thread. Every time Pakistan is beckoned with a crisis, she has been rescued by her guiding angels to let her live another day. While Pakistan's romance with US have lost its usual sheen, the country pitches desperate hope on its iron brother China. In the next chapter, I would dwell upon the centripetal forces or the glue that holds Pakistan together which impacts its future in a decisive manner.

Notes

1 Lieven, Anatol, 2011, "Pakistan: A Hard Country", New York: PublicAffairs, 2011.

2 Frances Pritchett, "Now or Never, by Chaudhary Rahmat Ali, 1933", https://franpritchett.com.

3 Barbara Metcalf, Thomas Metcalf, 2012, "A Concise History of Modern India", Cambridge University Press.

4 Muhammad Ahsan Jahangir, 2019, "Pakistan's National Identity Conundrum: Making Sense of the Composition, Evolution and Conflict of Pakistan's National Identity", https://bora.uib.no/bora-xmlui/bitstream/handle/1956/20057/Master-s-Thesis –

Muhammad-Ahsan-Jahangir.pdf.

5 J Sai Deepak, Bloomsbury India, 2022, "India, Bharat and Pakistan: The Constitutional Journey of a Sandwiched Civilization".

6 K. K. Aziz, 1993, "*The Murder of History: A Critique of History Textbooks Used in Pakistan*", Vanguard Books.

7 Ibid.

8 Tariq Rahman, 1996, "Language and Politics in Pakistan", Oxford University Press.

9 Tilak Devasher, 2016, "Pakistan: Courting the Abyss", HarperCollins India.

10 Muhammad Ali Jinnah, "Speech to the First Constituent Assembly of Pakistan, Karachi, August 11, 1947 - In Speeches and Statements of Quaid-i-Azam Muhammad Ali Jinnah: 1947–1948", edited by Khurshid Ahmad Khan Yusufi, Karachi, Research Society of Pakistan, University of the Punjab, 1996.

11 Government of Pakistan, "The Constitution of the Islamic Republic of Pakistan, 1973", National Assembly of Pakistan, https://na.gov.pk/uploads/documents/1333523681_951.pdf

12 2023 USCIRF Annual Report on Pakistan, https://www.uscirf.gov/sites/default/files/2023-05/Pakistan.pdf.

13 Pakistan Bureau of Statistics, Population by Religion, 2017 Census, May 19, 2021, https://www.pbs.gov.pk/content/population-religion.

14 Government of Pakistan, The Constitution of the Islamic Republic of Pakistan, 1973, https://na.gov.pk/uploads/documents/1333523681_951.pdf.

15 "Ethnic, Language and Religion Maps of Pakistan", n.d, Urban Planning, Transport, Pakistan, https://adeelmohammad.weebly.com/main/ethinic-language-and-religion-maps-of-pakistan.

16 Government of Pakistan, Pakistan Penal Code (Act XLV of 1860), as amended in the 1980s under General Zia-ul-Haq's Islamization program (Sections 295–298C), Islamabad: Ministry of Law and Justice, https://pakistancode.gov.pk.

17 "What Role Does the State Play in Pakistan's Anti Shia Hysteria?", The Diplomat, September 2020.

18 Shah Meer Baloch and Hannah Ellis-Petersen, 2023, "Man Tortured and Killed in Pakistan Over 'Blasphemy", The Guardian, July 21, 2023, https://www.theguardian.com/world/2021/dec/03/pakistan-sri-lankan-man-priyantha-diyawadana-tortured-killed-alleged-blasphemy-sialkot.

19 Anwar Iqbal, "1,000 minority girls forced in marriage every year: report," Dawn, April 8, 2014, referencing the Movement for Solidarity and Peace in Pakistan.

20 A.H. Nayyar and Ahmad Salim, "The Subtle Subversion: The State of Curricula and Textbooks in Pakistan, Islamabad", Sustainable Development Policy Institute, 2003.

21 Government of Pakistan, Constitution (Second Amendment) Act, 1974, Amendments to Articles 106 and 260, Gazette of Pakistan, Extraordinary, Part I, 21 September 1974.

22 "120 Graves of Ahmadis Desecrated," Dawn, December 3, 2012, https://www.dawn.com/news/768765/120-graves-of-ahmadis-desecrated.

23 'Situation Report: Monitoring the Plight of Ahmediyya Community in Pakistan', nchr.gov.pk/wp-content/uploads/2024/04/Ahmadiya-Report.pdf.

24 International Crisis Group, The State of Sectarianism in Pakistan, 18 April 2005.

25 'Ethnic Groups of Pakistan', https://www.reddit.com/.
26 Smruti Pattanaik, "Why Separatist Politics Has Plagued Pakistan Since Its Inception", *Indian Express*, January 18, 2023.
27 "Budget allocation: Provincial breakdown and sectoral distribution", Hum News, June 13, 2024.
28 Iqbal Singh Sevea, 2021, "The Pashtun Question in Pakistan", South Asia Scan, Institute of South Asian Studies, https://www.isas.nus.edu.sg/wp-content/uploads/2021/01/South-Asia-Scan-Vol-10-Full-14.04.21.pdf.
29 Encyclopaedia Britannica, "Durand Line", London, Encyclopaedia Britannica, June 2025.
30 International Crisis Group, Merger of FATA with Khyber Pakhtunkhwa and the Abolition of the FCR, Brussels: International Crisis Group, 2018.
31 Al Jazeera, 2014, "Pakistan's IDPs Reach Record One Million", *Al Jazeera*, September 1, 2014, https://www.aljazeera.com/news/2014/9/1/pakistans-idps-reach-record-one-million.
32 Daily Excelsior, "Gilgit-Baltistan: A Forgotten Corner of Pakistan," Daily Excelsior, April 8, 2015, https://www.dailyexcelsior.com/gilgit-baltistan-a-forgotten-corner-of-pakistan/.
33 "Gilgit Baltistan Empowerment and Self Governance Order 2009: Constitutional package seems to fail in meeting long standing demands", Business Recorder, August 31, 2009.
34 "Pakistan to Criminalise Enforced Disappearances", Deccan Herald, August 30, 2021, https://www.deccanherald.com/world/pakistan-to-criminalise-enforced-disappearances-1025195.html.
35 Human Rights Commission of Pakistan, "Dire Need for Better Governance and Accountability: HRCP Launches Fact-Finding Report on Rights Violations in Northern Sindh", Karachi: HRCP, September 8, 2023.
36 "World Sindhi Congress stages protest against Musharraf outside U.K. PM's residence", Business Standard, August 29, 2017.
37 Encyclopaedia Britannica, "German Militarism," last modified June 2025.
38 Philip K. Oldenburg, "India, Pakistan and Democracy", Washington, DC: Woodrow Wilson Centre Press, 2010.
39 PK Upadhyay, 'Radicalisation of the Pakistan Army', IDSA (October 2011).
40 "Faith in arms- General Zia-ul-Haq's Islamisation of Pakistan's Army has lessons for India", https://www.telegraphindia.com/opinion/faith-in-arms-zia-ul-haqs-islamisation-of-pakistans-army-has-lessons-for-India.
41 S.K. Malik, "The Quranic Concept of War", Lahore: Services Book Club, 1979.
42 Government of Pakistan, White Paper on the Jammu & Kashmir Dispute, Islamabad: Ministry of Foreign Affairs, Government of Pakistan, 1976.
43 Declan Walsh, 2017, "Pakistan army officer held over suspected Hizb ut-Tahrir links", The Guardian, November 26, 2017.
44 Ayesha Siddiqa, "Military Inc.: Inside Pakistan's Military Economy", Karachi: Oxford University Press, 2007.
45 Encyclopaedia Britannica, "List of Prime Ministers of Pakistan", Updated June 2025.
46 "The Struggles of the Pakistani Economy – Michigan Journal of Economics." 2024. April 17, 2024. https://sites.lsa.umich.edu/mje/2024/04/17/the-struggles-of-the-pakistani-economy/.

47 S.A.K. Sherani, "Power sector challenges", Dawn, February 12, 2021.

48 Foreign Affairs, "Pakistan's Jihad Culture", Foreign Affairs, November 1, 2000.

49 Jamila Achakzai, "Pakistan: Why is the number of illegal madrassas rising?", https://www.dw.com/en/pakistan-why-is-the-number-of-illegal-madrassas-rising/a-63607470.

50 "World Bank Climate Change Knowledge Portal," n.d, https://climateknowledgeportal.worldbank.org/country/pakistan.

51 Abid Hussain, 2025, "Deadly Pakistan Train Hijack: What Happened, Who Was Rescued, What's Next?" Al Jazeera, March 13, 2025.

Chapter Four

The Centripetal Glues

"The Pakistan Army is the most powerful institution in the country, and in many ways the only functioning one."

—Christine Fair[1]

What Keeps Pakistan Together: 'The Centripetal Glues'

Despite the centrifugal forces that threaten to tear Pakistan apart, it has always managed to stay afloat. Pakistan has been able to exploit various leverages to remain relevant, whether it was playing up the perennial belligerence against India or its support to the US in GWOT. The support of its all-weather friend China is another important factor which has not allowed Pakistan to fail as a state in the past. Pakistan's behavior on the world stage is shaped by its security-centric outlook, especially its rivalry with India. While it actively engages in multilateral forums and narrative-building efforts, its foreign policy remains constrained by internal fault lines and dependence on external powers. It is therefore prudent to analyze the centripetal forces which holds Pakistan together inspite of many fissures discussed in the previous chapter.

The Islamic Factor

Pakistan is a country with the second largest Muslim population.[2] The country was infact created as an exclusive homeland for the Muslims. In times of crisis, such as political instability, economic hardship or social unrest, Pakistan has often turned to Islam as a unifying and deflective force. Political leaders and institutions frequently invoke religious sentiments to rally national unity and shift public focus away from governance failures. By framing challenges as threats to Islamic values or linking them to foreign conspiracies against the

Muslim world, the state has tried to redirect public discourse toward emotional and ideological concerns. Issues like Islamophobia or solidarity with Muslim, causes such as Palestine, are often emphasized during turbulent periods. Islam was used as a unifying force to rally the population during wartime, especially in 1965, with slogans like, "Jihad fi Sabeelillah" (struggle in the path of God). The politicization of religion has created a sense of solidarity among common citizens, reinforcing a collective identity that transcends ethnic and regional divisions in Pakistan.

Pakistan has often brandished its Muslim identity amongst the larger fraternity of Islamic nations emphasizing the historical, cultural and religious bonds that it shares with them. Pakistan's ties with countries like Turkey, Saudi Arabia and UAE are often underpinned by Islamic solidarity besides convergence of economic and strategic interests. Pakistan is also the founding member of the OIC.[3] Pakistan's role in the OIC is central to its foreign policy and Islamic identity. It actively participates in all forums and committees of OIC, including the various contact groups. Pakistan has actively leveraged OIC to build alliances and support to further its foreign policy objectives. In the ongoing economic crisis, the gulf countries especially Saudi Arabia was the first to rescue Pakistan with an estimated aid of almost $ 5 billion in either deposits or roll over of debts.[4] Pakistani leaders – from Zulfikar Ali Bhutto to Imran Khan – have tried to use Islamic themes of unity (Ummah) to advocate for a stronger political bloc of Muslim-majority nations. The recent trend of OIC members cozying up to India has drawn consternation from Pakistan, which views this development as detrimental to her interest. Still, Pakistan remains one of the top five most active and agenda-setting members of the OIC.[5]

As the only Muslim country with nuclear capabilities, Pakistan holds a certain degree of influence within the Muslim world. Many Muslims around the world see Pakistan's nuclear capability as a symbol of power and pride. This status has elevated its symbolic and strategic significance among Islamic nations, positioning it as a potential deterrent force and a source of pride for many in the Muslim world. Often seen as a 'nuclear shield' for the Ummah, Pakistan's nuclear capability represents both scientific achievement and military strength.[6] While Pakistan avoids framing its nuclear arsenal in explicitly religious terms, its power projection and diplomatic influence within Islamic organizations like the OIC have been strengthened by this capability. This role also comes with responsibility and scrutiny, requiring Pakistan to balance its national interests with the expectations of broader Islamic solidarity. It is however dichotomous that inspite of the fact that Pakistan is the sole nuclear power amongst the Islamic countries, it finds it difficult to claim its rightful place amongst the comity of Muslim nations. Nonetheless, nuclear status is a binding factor for Pakistan and the larger Islamic fraternity which establishes technological and military prowess of Pakistan.

Another facet of Pakistan's relation with the Islamic world is the military engagement with Muslim countries spreading across multiple domains. Pakistan has maintained strong military ties with several Islamic countries, making it a key defence partner in the Muslim world. Its armed forces have provided training, strategic support, and personnel to countries such as Saudi Arabia, the United Arab Emirates, Qatar and Jordan. Pakistani military advisers and troops have been stationed in the Gulf, especially in Saudi Arabia, for decades, contributing to regional security and strengthening bilateral ties.[7] Pakistan also plays an active role in joint military exercises with various Muslim nations, reflecting its commitment to Islamic military cooperation. Additionally, Pakistan has trained officers from over a dozen OIC countries at its military academies, reinforcing its position as a trusted and capable military partner within the Islamic world.

While Islamic solidarity is a significant factor, Pakistan's foreign policy is ultimately driven by its national interests, which may sometimes deviate from the interests of other Muslim countries. Sectarian differences within the Muslim world pose a significant challenge to Pakistan's efforts in forging unified position like in the case of Iran which has a history of complex relationship with the entire Muslim world. Irrespective of this fact, Pakistan strategically employs its Islamic identity as a key leverage in its foreign policy. While national interests remain paramount, the shared religious heritage act as an ideological bridge between Pakistan and the rest of Islamic world. Pakistan has leveraged Islamic values and victimhood to deflect attention from its widening fault lines while continuously endeavouring to cement its status as a credible soft power in the Muslim world.

Guardian Angels

The second most important factor which has kept the country going are the so called Guardian Angels which are countries that have greater interest in Pakistan. Saudi Arabia has been cultivating Pakistan to remain a hegemon in Muslim world and so has been the reason for Turkey trying to snuggle up to Pakistan.[8] While the US desires to prevent Pakistan from falling into the Chinese hands, China on the other hand nurtures and supports Pakistan to develop it as a proxy against India. Today, Pakistan wants to partake in China's success story and never misses an opportunity to parrot the iron brother relationship between Pakistan and China. However, each guardian angel has its own interest and compulsion in engaging with Pakistan dictated by global constraints and inherent national interests.

Pakistan has been piggy backing on US for long. Since the Cold War, Pakistan has strategically utilized its relationship with the US to bolster its economic and military strength, often in relation to its rivalry with India, which was seen as being aligned with the Soviet Union. Pakistan's strategic location in South Asia, particularly regarding Afghanistan and the border with Iran, has been a key factor in its ability to extract maximum dividend from the relationship. Departure of US from Afghanistan after termination of GWOT gave an impression that Pakistan has outlived its utility for US. However, the reality is that the position Pakistan occupies in the Islamic world and the region in specific would never let Pakistan exit from the sphere of US interest and engagement especially in an extremely volatile geo-political environment obtained in the region. Today, US-Pakistan relations are transiting through a phase of cautious recalibration, with both countries seeking a pragmatic balance after years of fluctuating ties. While the strategic partnership of the early 2000s – centered on counterterrorism – has weakened, recent engagements suggest a shift toward broader cooperation in areas like trade, climate resilience, energy, and regional stability. US remains interested in Pakistan's role in ensuring security in Afghanistan and curbing extremism, while Pakistan seeks American investment and support for economic recovery. The visible outreach by the United States towards Pakistan following Operation SINDOOR, exemplified by the unprecedented invitation extended to General Asim Munir to visit the White House, signals a renewed American interest in recalibrating ties with Islamabad.[9] Irrespective of the lingering mistrust, growing US ties with India and Pakistan's proximity with China, US would continue to be a major stakeholder in Pakistan and its future, capable of swinging its influence as necessitated by situation and consequences.

Pakistan and China's relationship has evolved significantly over the years, from a phase of initial neutrality to a deep strategic engagement, often described as 'higher than the mountains and deeper than the seas'. This relationship is fueled by mutual trust and shared interests which has led to extensive cooperation in the field of defense, economics and infrastructure development. Although Pakistan and China established their diplomatic relations in 1951, their formative years witnessed little interaction.[10] The border treaty of 1963 was a defining moment in Pakistan-China relations, further enhancing mutual trust. The 1965 Indo-Pakistan war further cemented the ties with China fully supporting Pakistan. Another important building block in the relationship was the 1966 decision to construct the Friendship or Karakoram Highway linking China's Xinjiang region with Gilgit-Baltistan in Pakistan.[11] Today, this highway serves as the main route for CPEC. In July 1971, Pakistan played a seminal role in facilitating US Secretary of State Henry Kissinger's visit to China which changed the tide in US-China relations. Through the 80s and 90s, Pakistan and China struck a convergent chord overcoming all their initial reservations. Pakistan's joining BRI and the construction of CPEC was a landmark development in Pakistan-China relations. Today Pakistan is the largest importer of Chinese military hardware. China has stood firmly alongside Pakistan in every crisis. Chinese behavior towards Pakistan is dictated more by its own economic interests and the imperative of keeping India, a rising power in the region, under check which is likely to persist in the foreseeable future.

Pakistan's engagement with Saudi Arabia is dictated more by cultural and religious ties than strategic interests. Being home to Mecca and Madina, the two holiest cities in Islam, Saudi Arabia plays a significant role in the Muslim world. As an Islamic country, Pakistan sees its relationship with Saudi Arabia as special. Post 1947, Pakistan and Saudi Arabia have maintained strong political, economic and cultural ties. Since the reign of King Faisal, Saudi Arabia has provided financial support to thousands of Pakistani madrassas. The Kingdom has come to Pakistan's rescue on many occasions, for example when Pakistan was under international economic sanctions after testing of nuclear weapons in May 1998.[12] In the recent period from 2014 to 2022, Pakistan received three Saudi financial aid packages totaling nearly $9.5 billion. Pakistan's relationship is also special with Saudi Arabia because of the large expatriate community making significant contribution to its economy through remittances. There are about 2.7 million Pakistanis living and working in Saudi Arabia.[13] Besides providing economic assistance, the Kingdom has also been generously helping Pakistan deal with humanitarian crises. Pakistan is among the Kingdom's prominent security and strategic partners. As a result, Pakistan's civil and military officials have repeatedly assured Saudi leaders that Pakistan will go to any length to protect Saudi Arabia. The Protocol Agreement of 1982 formalized bilateral security ties, allowing the Kingdom to request Pakistani soldiers if needed. During Iraq's invasion of Kuwait in 1990–1991, Pakistan had deployed its troops in the Kingdom to protect its territorial integrity.[14] Regular high-profile military-to-military exchanges and infrequent joint exercises have taken place between the two countries. India's increasing engagement with Saudi Arabia and other Gulf nations in the recent years indicate a broader shift in regional influence. However, the thread of Pakistan's relationship with the Kingdom is considerably strong which would not be critically impacted by transitory developments in the geo-strategic sphere.

Pakistan and Turkey enjoy a deep-rooted and multifaceted relationship characterized by strong political, cultural and strategic ties. Their bond is founded on shared historical experiences, Islamic values and mutual support on key international issues. Turkey has consistently supported Pakistan's stance on Kashmir, while Pakistan backs Turkey's position on Cyprus and other regional matters. The two countries share close defence and economic ties. Pakistan-Turkey signed the Preferential Trade Agreement in 2022, which aims to boost bilateral trade and investment.[15] Both countries are members of OIC and have often aligned on major international forums. Turkey's Ambassador to Pakistan recently announced that the Turkish consulate under construction in Karachi, would be Turkey's largest consulate anywhere in the world, symbolizing the importance of Turkish–Pakistani ties.[16] Pakistan is the second largest recipient of arms exports from Turkey. Turkey has been active in upgrading F-16s for Pakistan and has supplied Pakistan with advanced drones, including the Bayraktar, TB2 and Akinci. Pakistan has also signed a deal to procure corvettes and helicopters from Turkey. Turkey's diplomatic and strategic choices are shaped by the complexities of the geopolitical developments, its involvement in Syria, tensions with Russia and Iran, and also its eagerness to be close to the OIC. Ankara's economic interest in Pakistan cannot be ignored and it potentially sees Pakistan as connector to Asia to expand its exports. The current conservative and Islamic regime of Recep Tayyip Erdogan has shown a distinct inclination in support of Pakistan on ideological grounds which categorizes Turkey as a major support nation for Pakistan in the eventuality of a crisis.

Identifying Pakistan's guardian angels is not difficult, however in the complex paradigm of geo-politics and volatile security environment, it would be interesting to observe the behavior of sympathizers and the fence sitters in a situation of catastrophic crisis in Pakistan. It is also a fact that India today has emerged as a promising regional power and a global voice of significance. It has also effectively extended its diplomatic outreach into the Muslim world which was historically considered belligerent to Indian interests. This changed perspective would impact the response and conduct of Guardian Angels who would be cautious and measured in their behaviour while dealing with Pakistan. Nonetheless, reasonable assurance of the support of these well-wishers or so called interested parties places Pakistan in a position of reasonable confidence to tackle a crisis, whether extrinsic or internal.

Animosity against India

Pakistan is a state which has always professed an institutional animosity or hatred for India, germinating from a sense of unfair partition. Separation of East Pakistan and creation of Bangladesh only cemented this sentiment which has now been permanently etched in the history of the nation. The fabricated idea of two nations, one Muslim and another Hindu which cannot cohabit, fuels this perception. For many years now, powers that have been in Pakistan, whether military dictators, Islamists or political personalities, everyone has indulged in this idea to serve own selfish interest. The recent rant of Pakistan Army COAS on 17 April 2025 while addressing the Pakistani diaspora is evidence of this deep-rooted consternation against India which unfortunately is also shared by a large majority of population in Pakistan.[17] It is from this perspective that a perennial belligerence against India is identified as a factor which would unite Pakistan in situation of crisis.

The Pakistani establishment has fuelled this belligerence against India in a systematic manner taking recourse of religion and history. Pakistan has framed India as a Hindu-majority adversary, reinforcing a narrative of religious opposition. Over time, this ideological foundation have deepened through state-controlled education and media, which often portrays Hindus and India in a negative light, shaping public perception from a young age. Pakistan's support for Islamic terrorist groups, since the 70s has encouraged religious extremism directed against India in particular which is often framed as holy war against non-Muslims. These strategies have hardened the negativity against India wherein it is often framed as an excuse for all internal woes of Pakistan. The other facet of false narrative is the perception that partition was an unfair division wherein Pakistan was denied its rightful share by India. Many in Pakistan believe that certain Muslim-majority areas were unfairly given to India. The division of Punjab and Bengal along religious lines, despite mixed populations, caused immense upheaval and violence.[18] Many in Pakistan believe that the division of assets and territory was skewed in India's favor leaving Pakistan with a weaker industrial base and economic structure as compared to India. In Pakistan's opinion it received a smaller share of the military and financial resources of British India. This initial deprivation is often cited in narratives of injustice. Pakistan led by its Army thus harbors a revisionist sentiment against India persistently challenging the status quo. This very perception has been capitalized by Pakistan Army and the political dispensation to aggregate the public opinion against India from time to time and in crisis.

Pakistan also uses belligerence towards India to justify its military spending, maintain strong ties with allies like China and present itself as a counterbalance to Indian influence in South Asia and beyond.[19] These factors, often reinforced by political leaders, the military establishment and religious groups, help sustain a national narrative of victimhood and resistance which Pakistan leverages for both domestic cohesion and international diplomacy. Today India is progressing on a fast trajectory of growth and development. As a potential challenge to China in the region, emergence of India has triggered a volatile contest in the regional geo-political environment. Pakistan sees itself as a counterbalance to India in South Asia by leveraging strategic alliances, military strength and ideological narratives. It presents itself as a key player in regional security and a bulwark against Indian dominance. Through its nuclear weapons program,

Pakistan has sought strategic parity with India despite economic disparities. It has also championed causes like Kashmir in international forums, aiming to challenge India's regional image and influence. Additionally, Pakistan has supported regional Islamic solidarity and aligned with groups or countries that oppose Indian policies, portraying itself as the voice of Muslim interests in South Asia. These efforts are part of a broader strategy to maintain relevance and strategic leverage in a region where India holds significant demographic, economic and geopolitical weight. Pakistan's attempt to assume a position of strategic counterbalance against India is also an important factor which would force the larger global community to rally behind Pakistan in a situation of crisis of depredation.

Overall, Pakistan views the intrinsic hatred for India and everything that India stands for as an advantage to amalgamate public opinion. This perspective has been exploited unabashedly by the Pakistan Army to retain a position of relevance and strength in the affairs of the state. The image of holier than the cow lends Pakistan Army the status of an institution that is insulated against any criticism or inquiry. When we talk about Pakistan's resilience to a critical situation, this factor of anti-Indianness ranks highest in the precedence which would be capitalized to meet the desired ends. The recent terrorist attack against innocent tourists in Pahalgam (UT of J&K) on 22 April 2025 and the rhetoric generated in its aftermath by the Pakistan Army is a livid example of Pakistan's tendency of shifting the balance of blame to India and its alleged design of suppressing Pakistan into submission.[20] For a nation fuelled by a religious rhetoric and historical hatred for decades, there cannot be any other better excuse or opportunity for externalizing their internal problems.

Pakistan Military

Pakistan Army has always remained the most important stake holder in the affairs of the state. The early demise of Mohammad Ali Jinnah created a void in the political landscape of Pakistan which was conveniently occupied by Pakistan Army. It has frequently portrayed itself as the only 'Saviour of Pakistan' and has imposed its leadership during various crises faced by the country.[21] Leveraging the perennial belligerence against India, Pakistan Army has effectively consolidated its stature and influence in Pakistan, deeply impacting the psyche of the civil society. With a stake in every facet of governance, it has grown in strength over the years. It may appear that the stature of Pakistan Army is diminishing post the recent political turmoil in the country, however the tutelary status of Pakistan Army is still strong and far from any challenge in foreseeable future. Crushing the spirit of PTI with the imprisonment of Imran Khan and the coercion of puppet government to approve a constitutional amendment extending the tenure of Pakistan Army COAS are testimony of the sweeping influence and power wielded by Pakistan Army.

It is often said that Allah, Army and America are the three tenets of Pakistan's stability.[22] While America might be on its way out being replaced by China, but Army and Allah are still strong pillars of Pakistan's existence. Since creation of Pakistan in 1947, army has evolved into one of the most influential institutions in the state, shaping not only security policy but also foreign relations, domestic politics and even the economy. This prominence stems from a combination of historical legacies, perceived security threats, and the military's own institutional strength and discipline. Politically, the Army has directly governed Pakistan for nearly half of its existence through military coups and seizure of power by military dictators. Even when the Pakistan Army is not in power, the military has exerted considerable control, often referred to as the 'establishment' in political discourse. Civilian governments are frequently seen as pawns in the hands of Army operating under the shadow of the military. In terms of foreign policy, the Pakistan Army – and particularly the ISI wing has played a pivotal role. Army explicitly controls foreign and defense matters exhibiting significant power in functioning of the state. It's a stranglehold that has resulted in a democracy where no prime minister has ever completed a five-year tenure, but three out of four military dictators managed to rule for more than nine years each.[23]

Economically, the military runs a vast network of business enterprises through organizations like the Fauji Foundation, Army Welfare Trust and National Logistics Cell.[24] These institutions control sectors ranging from agriculture and banking to real estate and manufacturing, giving the Army a powerful stake in the economy. Critics argue that this economic entrenchment not only gives the military financial independence but also incentivizes it to maintain its influence over national policy. Dr. Ayesha Siddiqa, a prominent Pakistani political scientist and former civil servant, provides an in-depth analysis of Pakistan Army's economic ventures in her seminal work, *Military*

Inc.: Inside Pakistan's Military Economy. As per her estimate, Pakistan's military business refereed by her as Milbus accounts for an estimated value of approximately $20 billion.[25] This obviously is without factoring the huge proportion of drug money in which Pakistan Army has a significant stake. Civilian institutions such as the Auditor General of Pakistan or parliamentary committees have minimal oversight over military-run businesses. This opacity fuels concerns about corruption, inefficiency, and the unchecked concentration of wealth and influence in the hands of a few.

Socially, the army enjoys a position of power and influence. The Pakistan Army feeds on the mirage of perpetual existential threats, both real and imagined, to maintain its outsized influence over the country's political and economic systems. For decades, the military has positioned itself as the sole guardian of national integrity, cultivating narratives of imminent external aggression, particularly from India and internal chaos that only it can contain. This manufactured sense of siege justifies its interventions in civilian governance, its control over vast business enterprises and its suppression of dissent. Public discourse is carefully molded to align with the military's version of national interest. The mirage persists not because it reflects reality, but because it serves power. Pakistan Army is often seen as the last bastion of respect and trust in an environment of corrupt civilian politicians. This perception, along with its control over media narratives, has helped the military maintain its legitimacy and deflect criticism, even amid growing calls for democratic reform and civilian supremacy.

In summary, the Pakistan Army wields comprehensive power in the country, blurring the lines between military and civilian domains. Its dominance in politics, policy, and the economy has made it a central, if not controversial pillar of the Pakistani state. While some see this as a source of stability, others view it as a fundamental obstacle to the country's democratic evolution and institutional balance. This power grants Pakistan Army the status of a force which can rally a nation to a cause undermining dissident voices while driving a global narrative of consolidation and united public opinion. This is an extremely important characteristic of Pakistani state which cannot be overlooked while debating the factors that define stability or vulnerability of Pakistan to stresses and pressures of identified faultlines.

Why the World won't give up on Pakistan?

In the preceding paragraphs I have endeavoured to put across important arguments in favour of strengths and catalysts which would prevent the descent of Pakistan into chaos in a situation of crisis. Most of these factors germinate from innate characteristics of Pakistan. It is also important to debate whether the world would give up on Pakistan in a moment of catastrophe or stand by it to help it survive. Pakistan has historically played a role in maintaining the balance of power in Asia, especially in South Asia. Pakistan is the only Muslim-majority country possessing nuclear weapons. The international community has a vested interest in ensuring the security and non-proliferation of these weapons. A failing state could raise serious concerns about the control and safety of its nuclear arsenal. Pakistan is the only Muslim-majority country possessing nuclear weapons. The international community has a vested interest in ensuring the security and non-proliferation of these weapons. A failing state could raise serious concerns about the control and safety of its nuclear arsenal. The failure of a large, strategically located country like Pakistan could have a destabilizing domino effect on the entire region, potentially leading to increased extremism, terrorism and cross-border conflicts.[26] Amidst all this China which has committed huge stake in Pakistan would not let Pakistan crumble without making an earnest attempt.

Conclusion

It is almost certain that the world does not wish Pakistan to fail due to its pivotal geopolitical location, the critical issue of nuclear security and the far-reaching negative consequences its failure could have on regional and global stability. However, the fault lines that have been discussed cannot be overlooked under a notion of global intent and likely indulgence. The contest between the centrifugal fault lines and the centripetal forces would be played out in the backdrop of global geo-political situation and the severity of internal crisis in Pakistan. What trajectory would Pakistan adopt in the near future would depend upon its capacity to remain relevant while managing the internal environment. In the next chapter, I would discuss the plausibility of various scenarios that can emerge in Pakistan given the fragility of the nation to various fault lines.

Notes

1 C. Christine Fair, 2014, "Fighting to the End: The Pakistan Army's Way of War", New York: Oxford University Press.

2 Jcoleman and Jcoleman, 2025, " Muslim Population Change", Pew Research Center, June 17, 2025, https://www.pewresearch.org

3 https://oic-oci.org accessed on 10 Apr 25.

4 PTI, 2024, "Increasing Deposits in Pakistan's Central Bank Among Saudi Arabia's USD 5 Billion Plan: Report", The Indian Express, April 10, 2024.

5 Aiman Iqbal, 2022, "Press Briefing on OIC by MOFA Pakistan - TDI", The Diplomatic Insight, March 24, 2022, https://thediplomaticinsight.com.

6 David Albright and Holly Higgins, 2003, "A Bomb for the Ummah", Bulletin of the Atomic Scientists, https://doi.org.

7 Talat Masood, 2022, "Pakistan's Military Diplomacy and the Middle East", Arab News, August 1, 2022, https://www.arabnews.com.

8 Zahid Shahab Ahmed, 2018, "Understanding Saudi Arabia's Influence on Pakistan: The Case of the Islamic Military Alliance to Fight Terrorism", https://doi.org.

9 Anwar Iqbal, 2025, "Pakistan Reclaims Strategic Space in Washington", *dawn.com*, June 22, 2025. https://www.dawn.com.

10 Li Qingyan, "China-Pakistan Iron Brotherhood: 70 Years Hand in Hand", https://www.ciis.org.cn/english/commentaries.

11 Muhammad Ali Shaikh, "Infrastructure: The Karakoram Connection," *dawn.com*, December 1, 2024, https://www.dawn.com/.

12 Bruce Riedel, "Saudi Arabia: Nervously Watching Pakistan," Brookings, January 28, 2008, https://www.brookings.edu/articles/saudi-arabia-nervously-watching-pakistan.

13 Abdul Shakoor Shiekh, "Pakistani Expats Have Contributed to Saudi Arabia's Development, Growth and Prosperity, Says Diplomat," Arab News, March 23, 2018, https://www.arabnews.com.

14 "Pakistan and the Saudi-led Anti-terror Coalition: Regional Implications for the Appointment of Gen. Raheel", https://studies.aljazeera.net.

15 "Pakistan, Turkiye Ink Preferential Trade Agreement," Global Affairs - International Magazine, August 13, 2022, https://globalaffairs.com.pk/2022.

16 Daily Sabah. "Turkey Inaugurates New Consulate in Pakistan's Karachi", January 14, 2021, https://www.dailysabah.com/politics/diplomacy/turkey-inaugurates-new-consulate-in-pakistans-karachi.

17 India Today, "Pakistan Army Chief General Asim Munir Speaks at Overseas Pakistanis Convention", April 17, 2025.

18 Kamakshi Ayyar and Abhishyant Kidangoor, "How The Memory of India's Traumatic Partition Is Being Preserved Across Borders," TIME, August 15, 2018, https://time.com.

19 Letters to the Editor, "A Ceasefire Is a Start. But India and Pakistan Still Face Huge Problems", The Washington Post, May 10, 2025, https://www.washingtonpost.com/opinions.

20 India Today, "Pahalgam Terror Attack Rhetoric by Pakistan Army Highlights India-Blame Strategy", April 22, 2025.

21 Reuters, "Beloved Strongman: Support for Pakistan Army Chief Surges After India

Conflict," US News & World Report, May 21, 2025, https://www.usnews.com/news.

22 Armaan Bhatnagar, "Allah, Army and America: How They Dictate Pakistan's Politics," The Times of India, April 17, 2022, https://timesofindia.indiatimes.com.

23 Al Jazeera, "No Pakistani Prime Minister Has Completed a Full Term in Office," Al Jazeera, April 9, 2022, https://www.aljazeera.com.

24 Janina Conboye and Humza Jilani, "How Pakistan's Military Is Taking Over Its Economy," Financial Times, January 28, 2025, https://www.ft.com.

25 Ayesha Siddiqa, "Military Inc.: Inside Pakistan's Military Economy". London, Pluto Press, 2007.

26 Washington Post, "An Alarming South Asia Powder Keg", May 20, 2025.

Chapter Five

Assessment of Future Scenarios

"May you live in interesting times- goes an old saying often attributed to the Chinese. While many people use the phrase casually to describe events in many countries, for Pakistan 'interesting times' are almost a constant fact of life."

—Laila Bokhari[1]

Analysis of fault lines in the previous chapter has given important insights into various vulnerabilities of Pakistan. Study of the country also brings out certain facets which can lend long term strength and stability to the nation, only if capitalized with a strategic vision. In the interest of India's growth as a developed country by 2047 it is pertinent to assess the joint impact of fault lines as well as galvanizing factors on the future of Pakistan which would impact India's strategic engagement with the western neighbour. Today, according to the Bank for International Settlements, the global economy is at a 'pivotal moment' – buffeted by protectionism, fragmented supply chains, slumping productivity and financial fragility arising from inflation and debt. Overlapping this economic turbulence is the increasing trend of securitizing economic domains turning trade, value chains and capital flows into urgent national security concerns. Together, these forces place the world in a period of extreme flux under duress, as international relations become ever more securitized.[2] Under the present circumstances which are likely to extrapolate for next few years, it is extremely difficult to prognosticate the future of volatile nations like Pakistan. Nonetheless, for the purpose of this study as also to keep the assessment within the parameters of pragmatism, identification of future scenarios as they may unfold in Pakistan has been restrained to next 10-15 years i.e. till 2035-40 which seems to be a fair time period.

Factors Influencing Future Scenarios

A country's future is shaped by a myriad of factors which includes global dynamics, internal turbulences, economic situation, political status, environmental changes, social trends etc. Understanding of these factors is important to arrive at plausible future scenarios which are relevant and correctly estimated. In case of Pakistan this exercise becomes more complex. It is a country of 169 million people, projected to grow to between 250 and 335 million by 2050, which would make it the fourth-or fifth-largest country in the world.[3] Whether Pakistan is geared to handle this implosion is suspect. Besides, it is riven by severe internal unrest and external pressures. Terrorism patronized as a state policy is rapidly becoming a domestic challenge with no enduring solution. Worse still, Pakistan is a nuclear state, which does not exude the confidence of the global community in safe custody of nuclear weapons. Apropos, where Pakistan is likely to be in the next ten years or so is a complicated question which is difficult to answer.

If we look at the history of Pakistan, it is a nation which has always been influenced by certain specific factors which have largely remained constant over the period of time which includes its fragile democracy, challenging economic situation and complex regional dynamics. Pakistan's democratic system is a farce which is remote controlled by its strong military. Recent events, such as the ouster and imprisonment of former Prime Minister Imran Khan, highlight the control of military over the functioning of civilian government. Pakistan's economy has been in a state of atrophy for many decades now, surviving on liberal and recurrent doles from financial institutions and international community. Pakistan's regional relationships, particularly with neighbours like India and Afghanistan, have remained ever complex and sensitive. Influence of China, as a major ally and a global power besides US continues to shape Pakistan's behaviour at the regional and international fora, potentially impacting both its internal and external dynamics.

William Milam, an American diplomat, and a senior policy scholar who served as Ambassador to Pakistan from 1998 to 2001, has identified six major variables which would influence the future course of Pakistan.[4] He describes 'Indian Centricity' of Pakistan's strategic thought process as the most significant factor which influences the behaviour of Pakistan. This emotion has not only been liberally exploited by successive governments (both political and military) but also leveraged to divert the attention of the population from repeated crises faced by Pakistan. The second factor is the relationship of Pakistan with 'Afghanistan' which has been marred by mutual distrust and reciprocal exploitation for several decades. Afghanistan was nursed to lend strategic depth to Pakistan however boisterous handling of the relationship today has turned Afghanistan as an 'Achilles Heel' for Pakistan in the geo-strategic space of South Asia. The third factor is the complex 'civil-military' balance in Pakistan which has been a permanent cause of consternation in the power circles of the state. Pakistan's experience suggests that the military invariably takes precedence in civil-military relations because the country was developed as a security state right from the early years due to fear of internal collapse. The space occupied by the military in the governance of the state has not been ceded till date. Influence of 'fundamentalism' especially amongst the youth and the society at large has been identified as the next challenge which has shaped the public narrative in Pakistan in the most significant manner. 'Economic Paradox' is both short term and long term factor in Pakistan's uncertain future. The last factor identified by William is the blow hot blow cold relationship that Pakistan has gotten to develop with US. Irrespective of Pakistan's growing closeness or dependence on China, US continues to remain an important stakeholder in the future of Pakistan.

Estimate of Future Global Environment

While contextualizing fault lines and dependent factors impacting the future of Pakistan, it is also important to identify the correct frame of reference to remain pragmatic. Obviously, black swan events like COVID-19 or even the economic recession of 2008 are difficult to predict but looking at the manner in which the geo-strategic environment is shaping up, one can make a fair assessment of the future construct. Today international relations are becoming increasingly complex. Challenge to a unipolar world with emergence of several multinational blocks has altered the behaviour of nation states. Arrival of Donald Trump on the scene and his aggressive manouvering to retain hegemonic control over the world affairs is bound to have ripple effect across complete global community.[5] The security environment is expected to become more volatile, with nations needing to navigate multifaceted risks. Important postulates of the assessed global environment in the near future are elaborated in the succeeding paragraphs.

China's rise has been the most defining event of the 21st century. China's rise as a global economic, technological and military power has profound implications for the world order, shifting the balance of power besides impacting international relations, trade, and global governance. This rise has also prompted both opportunities and challenges for various nations, including the US, Europe, India and obviously states like Pakistan. The Chinese view of the world is profoundly Sino-centric. US views China as its primary strategic competitor, leading to intensified rivalry across military, technological and economic domains. China's dominant role in supply chains, rare earths and market economy gives it the requisite tools for economic coercion. US and its allies are trying to reduce reliance on Chinese technology leading to a fragmented global ecosystem. China is also pushing for a more state-centric, authoritarian-friendly model of global governance, challenging liberal democratic norms.[6] Its growing assertiveness to assume the status of a global superpower amidst increasing friction with US on multiple domains would continue to impact the global dynamics through the century.

The rise of nationalism and protectionism has led to increased scrutiny of the positive impacts of globalization. A growing emphasis on national identity, sovereignty and often exclusionary politics has far-reaching implications for global security, diplomacy and international cooperation. While nationalism can foster unity and pride, its resurgence in many parts of the world is often linked with populism, protectionism and geopolitical tension. Factors like the COVID-19 pandemic and geopolitical conflicts have exposed weaknesses in global supply chains. Businesses remain interested in cross-border economic engagement, but the anti-globalization movement poses a threat to economic growth and international relations. Trump's transactional view of international politics represents a return to 19th century geopolitics and a rejection of all the lessons of the 20th century.[7] The transactional view of international relations puts no principle above pure national interest, but leads to failure of international cooperation in many respects. First, it represents a complete denial of the importance of international commitment. Secondly, it denies multilateralism and thirdly it undermines collective action at international level to common global challenges. Nationalism has also been leveraged as an excuse to distract attention from domestic problems or justify repression.

The most immediate threat to security in the coming decade would emerge from weak, failing and rogue states turning into safe haven for terrorist and criminal organisations. Unlike great power competition (like between US and China), the threats from these states are often more unpredictable, diffused and non-traditional – but still highly destabilizing. Failing states disrupt global markets by cutting off vital resources (like oil from Libya or Nigeria) or creating instability in key trade routes (e.g. piracy off Somalia or the Red Sea). Rogue states undermine international laws and norms by defying UN sanctions, sponsoring terrorism or engaging in illegal weapons programs. They challenge the credibility of global institutions, making enforcement of peace and security much harder. Their actions, such as aggressive military behaviour or interference in neighbouring countries, can destabilize entire region. Rogue states often disregard international agreements, undermining the global legal framework. Sanctions and countermeasures against these states can lead to global economic repercussions, affecting trade and energy markets.

Terrorism would continue to be a major risk for global security, though its nature has evolved. While large-scale attacks like 9/11 have become less frequent, terrorism still poses a persistent and adaptive threat with wide-reaching implications. Terrorist groups can erode state authority, especially in fragile or conflict-prone regions (e.g. ISIS in Syria and Iraq, Al-Shabaab in Somalia). They exploit ethnic, sectarian and political divide to deepen instability, provoke civil wars and hinder peace processes. Home grown terrorism is also a major concern – individuals radicalized online (without direct contact with terrorist organizations) can carry out attacks independently, threatening peace and security on a much larger scale. Impact of technological advances provide terrorist organizations new capabilities multiplying their lethality manifold. Continued diffusion of existing technology and knowledge would allow proliferation of Weapons of Mass Destruction and their means of delivery. Trans-national criminal organisations have become increasingly adept at exploiting disorder expanding the scope of its activities from drugs trafficking to services to terrorists.

Geopolitical risks have the potential to impact the global economic outlook, influencing growth, inflation, financial markets and supply chains. Current global economic challenges have far-reaching implications across various sectors and regions. Global growth is stabilizing at a modest rate of around 2.7% for 2025-26, which may not be sufficient to foster sustained development.[8] Trade policy shifts and geopolitical instability are major disruptive forces, affecting both global and regional economies. Many low and middle income countries are struggling with unsustainable debt, worsened by high interest rates and a strong dollar. Conflicts, such as the Russia-Ukraine war and the Israel-Hamas war, fuel regional instability and have impacted energy and food security, with higher prices leading to increased inflation rates. Fragile states are suffering disproportionately from global turbulences as they lack adequate financial buffer and often depend on aid and imports. Economic pressure can often exacerbate internal divisions, weaken governance and contribute to state failure or collapse. Economic competition is intensifying strategic rivalries as a result nations are shifting toward economic nationalism and 'friend-shoring' (prioritizing trade with allies), fragmenting the global economy.[9] Institutions like the IMF, World Bank and WTO are likely to face greater credibility challenges, as their tools appear insufficient or too slow to address global and regional challenges.

Energy and climate change continue to be politically polarizing issues, with global progress notably lacking on the climate transition. The recent energy price shock in the wake of Russia-Ukraine conflict has catalyzed decarbonization efforts albeit to a limited extent. Effects of climate change are far-reaching, touching every aspect of life whether economic, political, social or environmental, aggravating existing vulnerabilities in both developed and developing countries. Rising temperatures, droughts, floods, hurricanes and wildfires are becoming more frequent and intense, which may lead to collapse of ecosystem, loss of biodiversity, desertification and rising sea levels. Climate-related disasters displace millions annually. The UN projects up to 200 million climate refugees by 2050.[10] Climate change exposes inequities in global governance, with calls for climate justice, loss and damage funds, and debt relief gaining traction. Today, climate change is not just an environmental issue, it is a global systemic risk affecting peace, prosperity, health and stability. It challenges economic models, governance systems and global cooperation.

The global risk of perception operations, also known as information operations, cognitive warfare, or influence campaigns – has become a major threat to global security in the digital age. These operations aim to manipulate how individuals, societies, or governments perceive reality, often to achieve political, strategic, or ideological objectives without traditional warfare. These operations target elections, referendums, and public debates, often spreading disinformation to polarize voters or delegitimize results. State actors use perception ops as tools of hybrid warfare, shaping narratives before or during conflicts. Non-state actors (e.g. terrorist groups like ISIS) use slick online content to radicalize and recruit. These tactics are cheap, deniable, and highly effective at sowing chaos or gaining strategic leverage. Cyber-attacks are becoming more frequent and severe, and the human and financial impact of attacks continues to rise in line with the increasing digitization of critical infrastructure. Cyber warfare represents a new frontier in global conflict, involving digital attacks aimed at disrupting, damaging or infiltrating another's critical infrastructure.

Overall, the unipolar dominance of US is giving way to a more complex multipolar world with rising powers like China and India and regional blocs gaining influence. The world is likely to experience more geopolitical competition, but also regionalism wherein nations would prioritize local alliances and self-interest over global cooperation. Institutions like the UN, WTO, and WHO may struggle to stay relevant unless reformed. The climate crisis will be a defining issue, intensifying extreme weather, food insecurity, migration, and water/resource conflicts. Truth and trust will be under constant attack as AI-enhanced disinformation, deep fakes, and perception operations grow more sophisticated. Societies may struggle with reality fatigue. Polarization could deepen unless mitigated by digital literacy and strong civic institutions. Future conflicts would be mostly non-traditional characterized by cyber-attacks, space warfare, economic coercion and climate-driven resource disputes.[11] Gray Zone Warfare would blur the lines between war and peace. States would invest more in resilience, misinformation defence and hybrid warfare readiness. Democracies across the world are likely to face internal challenges from populism, disinformation and erosion of institutions. The future global environment would be dynamic, interconnected and increasingly volatile – marked by climate pressure, technological disruption, shifting power structures and the fight for truth. It would be a time of both unprecedented risk and limited opportunity.

Current Status of Pakistan

Having defined the likely global environment which would prevail in the near future, it would be prudent to audit the present status of Pakistan so as to arrive at a correct prognosis. With an economy which is declining, ethno-nationalism which has been existing for many decades, civil-military divide which dates back to the 1950s, terrorism which has become more of a way of life, food crisis which is unprecedented and the religious divide which is as old as the birth of Pakistan, accurate prediction of the future is still extremely difficult. Pakistan is dexterous in wading through troubled waters and emerging out of every crisis, however today the situation it is in is extremely precarious.

- **Depleting Credibility**. The world views Pakistan with suspicion. Identified as a global troublemaker, the previous US President, Joe Biden assertively called out Pakistan as a dangerous nation during one of his congressional campaign speeches in Oct 2022.[12] With the support of guardian angels and the allies diminishing, the world today has started considering Pakistan as more of a liability than an asset in Asia. Off late Pakistan's traditional friends have been circumspect, Taliban is not pliable and China is unbearably assertive. Even Saudi Arabia and UAE have been evasive to a large extent in bailing out Pakistan. The facade that Pakistan had very effectively created earlier as the saviour of the Muslim world is under scrutiny due to its own internal instabilities. The Judiciary-Executive-Legislative divide is increasing, which is also affecting the political stability of the country. Apprehensions of IMF and World Bank to commit resources coupled with fuel and power crisis, water deficiency, poverty, rise in illiteracy, gap between the haves and the have-nots and the adventurism of political parties have collectively dented the overall credibility of Pakistan.

- **Internal Security Situation.** The internal security situation in Pakistan is grim. The country has seen a rise in terrorist incidents, particularly in regions like Khyber Pakhtunkhwa and Baluchistan. Porous borders with Afghanistan and Iran have allowed militant groups to operate with relative ease, exacerbating security concerns. The Global Terrorism Index 2025 ranks Pakistan as the second most affected by terrorism globally, following Burkina Faso.[13] In 2024, terrorism-related deaths surged by 45% to 1081, with attacks more than doubling from 517 to 1099. TTP was responsible for over half of these casualties, carrying out 482 attacks that claimed 558 lives.[14] The insurgency in Baluchistan has intensified, with groups like the BLA conducting more sophisticated and deadly attacks, including the hijacking of a passenger train recently and ambushes on security convoys. These actions are fuelled by longstanding grievances over resource exploitation and political disenfranchisement. The separatist groups have increasingly targeted Chinese nationals and projects under CPEC, viewing them as symbols of economic marginalisation. Political tensions remain high, with extremist groups exploiting the situation to further their agendas. Pakistan's plan to deport over 1.3 million undocumented Afghan refugees has led to humanitarian concerns, especially in regions like Khyber Pakhtunkhwa, where many Afghans have lived for decades and have deep cultural ties.[15] Despite launching several military campaigns over the years, including operations Zarb-i-Azb and Raddul Fasaad, the state has struggled to fully neutralise terror networks.[16] The current political instability is likely to further accentuate the internal security situation in Pakistan which hinges precariously in a critical state today.

- **Economic Imbalances.** Predominantly an agrarian economy, Pakistan has transitioned through various phases of growth and turbulence influenced by political developments in the country. Two distinct factors which have constantly impacted the economic situation in Pakistan are their continued reliance on foreign aid and the dominance of Pakistan Army in the affairs of the state. Pakistan today faces an unprecedented economic crisis marked by fast-depleting reserves, declining exports and remittances, surging inflation, rising unemployment, weakening currency and decreasing business production which threaten the country's financial stability and the well-being of its citizens. There are fundamental structural problems that have been responsible for Pakistan's persistent macroeconomic challenges and tend to compound the impact of extraneous factors. Pakistan Army's lien over the budget and ever burgeoning financial outlay has also drained the resources which have struggled to meet the fiscal requirements. In the last several decades. Pakistan has approached the IMF for financial assistance 23 times since 1958, securing 13 formal bailout packages, and has frequently survived on the razor's edge of default.[17] However, weak monetary policies, lack of strategic planning and short-sighted approach of appeasement followed by regimes and governments in Pakistan has rendered the overall economic situation of Pakistan as extremely vulnerable impacting the stability of the country.

- **Politico-Military Turmoil in Pakistan.** The political landscape in Pakistan is characterized by deepening military dominance over civilian governance, escalating insurgencies and a fractured polity. Post arrest of Imran Khan on 09 May 2023, the unprecedented outburst and angst against Pakistan Army reflects the deep-rooted hatred harbored by the people of Pakistan for too long.[18] The myth of a sacred Army has definitely been dented but not completely broken. Pakistani Army continues to exert substantial influence over the nation's political affairs. Recent legislative changes, such as the extension of military Chiefs' tenures from three to five years, have been criticized for consolidating military power and undermining democratic processes.[19] High inflation, power shortages and dwindling foreign investments have exacerbated country's economic crisis. Military's involvement in economic councils, highlight its influence in specific facets of governance. The convergence of military dominance, escalating insurgencies, and political instability poses significant risks to Pakistan's national cohesion. Over a period of time there has been an erosion of democratic institutions in Pakistan coupled with human rights concerns and economic challenges which leaves Pakistan in an uneasy situation.

- **Energy Crisis.** Today Pakistan is grappling with a grim and critical energy crisis. Pakistan's power sector is burdened by a circular debt exceeding PKR 2.39 trillion.[20] This debt cycle, fuelled by poor governance, inefficient management and outdated policies, hampers the financial viability of energy providers and leads to frequent power outages. Outdated transmission and distribution systems result in significant technical losses and frequent load shedding, particularly in rural areas. These inefficiencies increase operational costs and reduce the reliability of power supply. The country is heavily dependent on imported fossil fuels, making it vulnerable to global price fluctuations and supply disruptions. In 2024, 59% of Pakistan's electricity was generated from fossil fuels, while only 2.7% came from wind and solar sources.[21] Addressing the energy crisis in Pakistan is a complex and challenging task, however recent discovery of fresh oil and gas reserves in western region of Pakistan may ease out the pressure on energy sector.

Overall, Pakistan is navigating a complex landscape marked by economic trepidations, security challenges and regional tensions. Economically, the nation is implementing stringent measures under a $7 billion IMF program, including job cuts, ministry dissolutions and new taxes, aiming to stabilize its financial situation.[22] On the security front, the country continues to face threats from terrorist groups with a restive Baluchistan and Khyber Pakhtunkhwa. Pakistan is grappling with the deportation of over 1.3 million undocumented Afghan refugees; a move met with resistance in regions like Khyber Pakhtunkhwa due to cultural and logistical challenges. Domestically, public sentiment is stirred by international events, with significant protests organized by groups like Jamaat-e-Islami reflecting the nation's engagement with broader geopolitical issues. Pakistan faces new security challenges today emanating from shifting global power dynamics with intensifying US-China power competition, growing Indo-US strategic partnership, unending cycle of violence in restive provinces, advancing technology and cyber threats, changing geopolitics in the region, and emerging trans-boundary terrorism from Afghanistan.

Likely Future Scenarios

Having analysed the existential fault lines in Pakistan and the likely global as well as regional environment over the next decade, there are three different scenarios for Pakistan appreciated to unfold in the future. Pakistan may either remain functional gradually improving across all developmental indices or become more fragile finding it difficult to grapple with a rapidly deteriorating situation. The third and most dangerous scenario could be a fragmented Pakistan with at least Baluchistan and Khyber Pakhtunkhwa breaking away to exist as independent regions. The three scenarios are elaborated in the succeeding paragraphs.

Functional Pakistan

It is not difficult to envision a functional Pakistan. Although from a realistic perspective and given the current state of affairs in the country, one has to be cautious while drawing the picture of a functional Pakistan. A diagnostic assessment of Pakistan indicates five specific issues that would have to be fixed for Pakistan to function reasonably which are political stability, economy, law and order/Internal Security, social harmony and environmental sustainability.

- **Pakistan's political landscape** is complex. Right from the time Pakistan was created, it has been plagued with political infirmity and lack of a clear vision. Pakistan's political system has identified itself more with political leaders, that too far and few, rather than inculcating a political ideology. The spaced ceded by polity has been captured by the military which has progressively cemented its influence. As a consequence, there can be no political discourse in Pakistan today without endorsement of Pakistan Army. Emergence of Imran Khan and PTI's rise to prominence has changed the political milieu in Pakistan.[23] The other political players are either marginalized or resigned to a fate of compromised compliance. Imran Khan's popularity resonates with the masses. Today, there cannot be a political solution without participation of Imran Khan in the process. A functional Pakistan would thus necessitate a purposeful understanding between Imran Khan and Pakistan Army for a viable political process to take place.
- **Pakistan's economy** suffers from a congenital challenge. It never had a strong foundation or clear vision and always served the short term aspirations of successive populist regimes whether civil or military. In the initial years, economic prudence was highjacked by strong feudalists who were more concerned in securing their turf as well as profits rather than investing in building a formidable economy. Advent of military dictators infused the fledgling economy with liberal foreign aids secured on the premise of an artificial threat from India.[24] In case that failed, the geo-strategic leverage was capitalized to keep the western powers invested and coffers filled. As a consequence, the economy suffered with weak institutions and immature federal practices. Pakistan's listing on the grey list recently was one of the biggest blows to its economy. Although with the last IMF bailout it is on its path of

recovery. Economic stability rests on continued support from financial institutions, donor countries and compliance with economic protocols legislated by IMF and World Bank without political or military interference. A functional Pakistan would have to manage these challenges efficiently upholding the confidence of her 'Guarding Angels'.

- **Internal security** of Pakistan is in doldrums. The current situation has arrived as a consequence of multiple failures on various accounts besides the arrogance of establishment to give due importance to each of them. Most of the lawlessness and violence emanates from the skewed federal balance in Pakistan and high headed handling of provinces by the centre. Punjabization of Pakistan politics has been called out for long. Whether it is Baluchistan, Khyber Pakhtunkhwa or for that matter Sindh or even Gilgit-Baltistan, the centre has always trivialized the grievances of people from these regions, fuelling discontent and desperation. Liberation groups like BLA and their associates in Baluchistan and the Pashtuns in Khyber Pakhtunkhwa have become powerful in their own turf and cannot be brushed aside. Federal reforms with due participation of all stakeholders is important for any semblance of stability in Pakistan. Sectarian violence, ethnic discontent, drug cartels, gang wars amidst widespread unemployment and an unmanageable youth bulge are other critical factors accentuating law and order in Pakistan which would have to be addressed through effective governance for a Functional Pakistan.
- The **society** in Pakistan is gradually becoming rabid with increasing intolerance and rising disgruntlement. The divide between rich and poor in an environment of rampant corruption and misgovernance has increased the desperation amongst the population. Proliferation of social media and increasing awareness amongst all sections of the society has made things worse. One of the major reasons for societal disharmony is the fact that Pakistan still finds it difficult to shake out of a feudalistic mindset.[25] Religious intolerance and a society which finds itself increasingly vulnerable to radical indoctrination makes the challenge more complex. Education especially amongst the lower middle class has suffered in the recent years. Mushrooming of

numerous madrassas which act as nurseries for radical organizations has marginalised the youth who feel more susceptible to the lure due to poverty, unemployment and lack of education. Scenario of a stable Pakistan is premised on the fact that concrete steps would be taken by the authorities to mitigate the vulnerabilities of the society and harness the demographic dividend existing in the country.

- Pakistan faces a range of environmental challenges that threaten its sustainable development and future trajectory. Climate change management, water scarcity, air pollution and deforestation are critical impediments to growth. Population implosion, unplanned urbanization and weak environmental governance further exacerbate these issues. Pakistan is highly vulnerable to climate change with rising temperatures, melting glaciers and unpredictable rainfall patterns leading to frequent floods and droughts. In 2022 floods Pakistan lost almost 1739 persons with an estimated damage of USD 40 billion.[26] Water scarcity is becoming critical due to inefficient management, while major cities suffer from hazardous air pollution levels. Deforestation and land degradation has increased the risk of desertification. To mitigate these challenges, Pakistan would need a multi-pronged approach through promotion of renewable energy, strict environmental regulations and improved waste management. Canaling of various rivers and fresh review of water sharing with India and Afghanistan are important pre-requisites to ensure water availability besides mitigating threat of destructive floods every year. It may be assumed that Pakistan is able to address all these besides strengthening institutional mechanisms to ensure environmental sustainability over a protracted period.

Overall, actualization of this scenario of a functional Pakistan is premised on the fact that Pakistan would be able to secure its interests while managing the vulnerabilities of critical fault lines. This cannot be accomplished till such time there is prolonged political stability internally and a positive engagement with the larger global environment to assuage the apprehensions on the future of the state.

Fragile Pakistan

Scenario of a fragile Pakistan is an extrapolation of the current state of affairs in the country marred by crippling institutions and continued degradation of global confidence in the state. Today Pakistan is navigating a complex landscape marked by economic challenges, political tensions, and security concerns amidst evolving regional dynamics. Description of a fragile Pakistan would entail ineffective diplomacy, political breakdown (or seizing of power by military), restive borders (Afghanistan, India and Iran), deterioration of law and order beyond civil control under conditions of economic collapse, threatening the very foundation of sovereign authority in the state.

- Pakistan's failure to leverage its assumed strategic identity is one of the most critical factors which would accelerate her descent into a state of anarchy and disorder. Pakistan's strategic identity is primarily derived from are its geo-strategic location and Muslim character. Pakistan has been leveraging these factors for long to secure its interests in every bargain. However with GWOT on the backburner and a global order shifting towards nationalism and self-interest, the leverage of Pakistan has diminished rapidly. In a state of fragile Pakistan, its flawed diplomacy to bargain both from the US as well as China has been unproductive, resulting in loss of critical strategic space it enjoyed in the region. In the comity of Muslim nations, Pakistan today is more of a reactive player than a leader. Pakistan is viewed in parts of the Muslim world as a country struggling with extremism and intolerance, especially toward minorities which hurts its image as a unifying Islamic voice. Pakistan has tried to leverage the OIC on issues like Kashmir, but these efforts have often result in tepid support. Countries like Saudi Arabia and the UAE have diversified their foreign policy and regional alliances in favour of self-interest. A state of extreme fragility would entail an isolated Pakistan which would not only be a threat to its own existence but also the security and stability in the region.
- Possibility of a political apocalypse in Pakistan is high. The public opinion on political matters is becoming increasingly critical with better awareness amongst masses. As in the past, fragility in the political space has always been exploited by military which considers itself as the custodian of the sovereignty of the state. Disbandment of PTI

and conduct of a sham election in Feb 2024 under the tutelage of Pakistan Army are indicators of distinct political manipulation undertaken with impunity.[27] But the fact that Imran Khan refuses to toe the Army line while commanding significant following across the country creates a situation with high risk of implosion. There have been very few instances when military in Pakistan has suffered a push back. One of that times was the public uproar post arrest of Imran Khan. Pakistan Army today has its hands full. The propensity of military to seize political power always remain high but under the present constraints and internal flux, the possibility of same remains considerably low. It is therefore highly possible that a situation triggered by any of the flash points spirals out of control leading to political breakdown which would render Pakistan extremely vulnerable. A scenario of fragile Pakistan implies political bankruptcy in a situation where military is reluctant to assume power, thereby propagating an environment of uncertainty and chaos.

- **Pakistan's borders** with its neighbours – India, Afghanistan, Iran and China, each have distinct dynamics, ranging from tense military standoffs to cautious cooperation. The Line of Control with India remains volatile, although there has been relative calm since a 2021 ceasefire agreement minus the abrasion during Operation SINDOOR. It's a fact though that diplomatic ties between India and Pakistan remains frozen, especially after India's revocation of Article 370 in 2019. Pakistan-Afghanistan border is highly porous and unstable. Pakistan has been fencing it over the past few years, which has caused diplomatic friction with the Taliban-led Afghan government which does not recognize the Durand Line as a legitimate border.[28] Frequent cross-border attacks by TTP has aggravated the situation. Pakistan has deported over a million undocumented Afghans recently, straining humanitarian and bilateral ties. Despite talks with the Afghan Taliban, Pakistan remains vulnerable to security threats emanating from across this border. Pakistan's border with Iran is prone to terrorist activity, particularly by Baloch separatist groups and smuggling networks. In January 2024, both countries exchanged airstrikes targeting each other's alleged terrorist hideouts, demonstrating the low threshold of violence along the restive border.[29] China's investment in CPEC and the growing discontent amongst the endemic Baloch population against the project has complicated the security situation in the province. Pakistan on a brink as visualized in this scenario would manifest with gradual deterioration of cross border situation both with Afghanistan and India stretching Pakistan military on both ends. Increased attacks on Chinese nationals and CPEC assets with greater collusively between Baloch separatists on either side of Iran border would only worsen the situation.

- **Internal unrest** in Pakistan could involve a convergence of political, economic, sectarian and security crises leading to widespread instability. The biggest threat to law and order in the country emerges from the failure of central establishment which has mostly exhibited inertia or at times utter disdain in responding to critical situations. If we paint a picture of internal turbulence, a scenario would emerge wherein civil-military confrontation would spiral out of control, with the military losing its grip or facing internal divisions. Widespread protests against perceived rigged elections or government overreach would be met with violent crackdown. Major sectarian riots (Sunni-Shia, etc.) erupt in key cities. Baloch separatists, Sindhi nationalists or Pashtun rights groups would escalate armed insurgencies. TTP and ISIS-K may exploit the chaos and retake territory in tribal regions or Khyber Pakhtunkhwa besides orchestrating major terrorist attacks in cities, key industrial infrastructure or even nuclear facilities. Return of foreign fighters or an influx from Afghanistan would heighten the threat. Karachi or other urban areas would descend into ethnic turf wars causing massive displacement of people. In such a situation, the foreign embassies would shut down or evacuate. Pakistan would come under global sanctions due to nuclear instability or human rights abuses. Neighbouring countries (especially India or Iran) may militarize borders against obvious threats. Pakistan's nuclear arsenal would become a major concern in this situation with the world concerned about their safety. The *worst case* is a systematic collapse similar to Libya or Lebanon, combined with the dangerous presence of nuclear weapons and a powerful but divided military, making the situation extremely precarious.

- The **economic situation** in Pakistan can worsen significantly if key risks are not addressed. The country is already on fragile ground, and several internal and external factors could tip it into a deeper crisis. Pakistan owes over $130 billion to the donors, with billions due annually in repayments.[30] If inflows (loans, remittances, exports) fall short, default becomes likely. If Pakistan fails to meet IMF conditions (tax reforms, energy price hikes, fiscal discipline), the program may be suspended or terminated. Without IMF support, other lenders (World Bank, ADB, and China) may also back off. Pakistan has a high debt-to-GDP ratio, with a significant portion of its debt owed to bilateral and multilateral creditors. This reliance on external borrowing creates a cycle of debt repayment, making it difficult to invest in productive sectors and manage the economy effectively. Political instability can create uncertainty for investors, hindering economic growth and attracting capital flight. Persistent fiscal deficits and external imbalances can lead to pressures on the currency and foreign exchange reserves, potentially triggering a crisis. Dwindling foreign exchange reserves make it difficult for Pakistan to meet its import needs and external debt obligations, further exacerbating the economic crisis. Events like the devastating 2022 floods in Pakistan caused immense economic disruption damaging critical infrastructure, halting agricultural and industrial production and severely impacting millions of livelihoods across the country.[31] Pakistan's economic fragility is a systemic issue, not a short-term problem. Without serious structural reforms, a worsening scenario is not only possible – it's likely. The situation is salvageable, but the window is narrowing.
- The scenario of fragile Pakistan is premised on a rapidly deteriorating situation with all instruments of power stretched beyond capacity of handling emerging crises. In this situation the fault lines are likely to become more pronounced leading to creation of multiple power centres. Steadily the country would reach the brink of fragmentation, more so if the anti-India sentiment fails to keep it united. With a fractured society and a dwindling economy, the country becomes fragile and divided but yet not fragmented. The situation may improve if China and US intervenes for their own vested interests. If not,

Pakistan would definitely progress towards a 'Lebanonised'[32] state of existence.

Fragmented Pakistan

The third scenario is based on the manifestation of a dangerous situation wherein very sovereignty of the state gets threatened. This situation would be premised on exacerbation of critical fault lines accentuated by both intrinsic and extrinsic factors leading to catastrophic failure. Pakistan's several power centres such as the military, political parties, religious groups and radical elements could become pawns to extra-regional players. Pushed around for strategic and ideological gains, Pakistan's capacity to influence its future would be reduced or become simply non-existent. The main factors which would lead to unfolding of this scenario are foreign interference, civil-military imbalance, economic collapse, ethnic separatism and rise of fundamentalist or terrorist groups.

- Pakistan since creation has been susceptible to foreign interference or influence. Pakistan adopted an identity of security state which perceives a threat to its national survival or danger to its sovereign existence resulting in a preponderant diversion of national resources towards security versus economic and social development. A security state inherently dictates the structure of a rentier economy, shaping its political, economic and institutional frameworks to prioritize military and strategic imperatives over productive economic development.[33] Since 1947, Pakistan has tried to bargain its geographical location, to align or promote great power geo-strategic goals. Initially US and lately China has served as an external pillar to the elitist, army-led and feudal-dominated idea of Pakistan. Pakistan's poor policy choices and endemic crisis of governance has made it overly dependent on external financiers like the US, Saudi Arabia and China who have their own strategic needs to feed upon. Today, US may no longer be the pillar of the system but it does remain a crutch, a potential strategic and financial threat.[34] China has been investing heavily primarily to offset its strategic constraints under the garb of iron brother. There is indeed a possibility of power play between the guardian angels of Pakistan who would go to any length in securing their interest in the region. In a scenario where the inherent fault lines become critical, interference from global powers could further accentuate the environment of uncertainty. They could exacerbate tensions between Pakistan and its neighbours, by supporting proxy groups or engaging in border provocations. Similarly, threat to CPEC or Chinese assets in Pakistan would impact China's involvement in the region. In a scenario of existential crisis in Pakistan, foreign actors would not only influence the institutions inside the country but also mobilize the world opinion in their interest.

- **Civil-military imbalance** is the biggest threat to cohesion of Pakistan as a sovereign state. Pakistan's history is replete with examples of how civil-military imbalance has negatively impacted the country. Repeated military coups have stunted democratic growth. Even during periods of civilian rule, the military has often wielded significant influence behind the scenes on key policy matters, particularly those related to security and foreign affairs. This has often led to tensions between civilian leaders and the military establishment. If elections are perceived as rigged or the judicial system collapses under pressure, faith in governance erodes. That could lead to unrest, regional autonomy movements or secessionist calls. Today, Pakistan Army has been pushed to the wall under a ternary stretch along the western and eastern borders while grappling with a rapidly deteriorating law and order situation in the restive provinces.[35] Handling of the Imran Khan situation both by the polity and the Army has been inadequate. Although Army continues to be a powerful institution in Pakistan, its influence is no longer absolute. In a scenario where the very existence of the state comes under threat, this imbalance would prove disastrous in recovering from the situation. The arrogance of Pakistan Army and its false- belief in power has systemically eroded the very foundation of Pakistan. As the widening fault lines exert pressure, Pakistan Army would deflect responsibility while the political fraternity would act as a mute spectator to the destruction of a flawed idea of Pakistan.
- **Economic crises** do not always cause fragmentation on their own, but they can severely weaken the state's capacity to govern, creating

fertile ground for ethnic, political, or external pressures to intensify and ultimately undermine national cohesion. Pakistan's debt-to-GDP ratio is high, and it relies on bailouts from the IMF, China, Saudi Arabia, etc.[36] If Pakistan defaults or fails to meet loan conditions (e.g., subsidy cuts, tax hikes), the rupee crashes, imports become unaffordable, and inflation spikes. A balance-of-payments crisis can lead to shortages of essential goods including fuel, food and medicine. Pakistan has already faced over 30% inflation in recent years. If climate change hits crops (especially wheat or cotton) or water availability drops, food insecurity can spark urban riots or even rural insurgencies. Power outages, energy shortages and lack of investment would hurt key sectors like textiles, agriculture and manufacturing. Economic grievances feed ethnic nationalism. Smaller provinces (like Baluchistan and Sindh) often argue that Punjab takes the lion's share of national resources. In a financial crisis, if federal funding dries up, these regions may push for autonomy or even independence. In an apocalyptic scenario, the course of crisis would entail collapse of IMF loan talks leading to fall of rupee thereby exploding inflation. Gradually public anger would grow; cities would face riots with breakdown of law and order. As provinces demand control of their resources, centre's control would diminish. Separatist and extremist groups would exploit the chaos. As military intervenes and grapples to regain control, there would be complete anarchy disorder threatening the very existence of the state.

- **Ethnic separatism** in Pakistan stems from deep-rooted grievance amongst various regional and linguistic groups who feel marginalized by the central government, particularly Punjabi-dominated powerful elites. Provinces like Baluchistan, Sindh and Khyber Pakhtunkhwa have witnessed varying degrees of separatist sentiment driven by perceptions of economic exploitation, political exclusion and cultural suppression. The Baloch insurgency is most active today with the highest probability of rapid implosion. Practically, ethnic tensions alone would not be adequate to affect disintegration of Pakistan, especially with a strong military. But when combined with economic collapse, political dysfunction and regional power imbalances, separatist movements can become powerful enough to threaten territorial unity. A scenario of continued exploitation of marginalized provinces and ethnicities would unfold with widespread resentment among people supported by armed groups especially in Baluchistan and Khyber Pakhtunkhwa. Accusations of Punjabi dominance in institutions and resource allocation would intensify, leading to a sense of disenfranchisement in most of the provinces. Separatist movements in Baluchistan, Sindh and Khyber Pakhtunkhwa would gain momentum, attracting more disillusioned youth. Provincial governments, backed by strong ethno-nationalist sentiment would begin to assert greater autonomy, challenging the federal government. Large-scale protests and acts of civil disobedience would erupt stretching the military and paramilitary forces. Emboldened by their growing strength and the central government's weakening grip, separatist movements in one or more provinces would declare independence. This conflict could draw in regional actors, further complicating the situation.

- **Fundamentalism** is a phenomenon synonymous with the character of Pakistani state. Politicisation of religion has rendered the society extremely polarized wherein faith has emerged more as a factor of division rather than holding the people together. The clergy has wielded considerable influcncc in Pakistan.[37] They have been exploited both by the Army and the political factions to aggregate power even at the cost of fragmenting the society. Today, Pakistan is transitioning through a phase of demographic advantage with a distinct youth bulge. Inability of the nation to harness this critical resource has pushed the youth towards radicalisation and in the lap of various Islamic organizations. Fundamentalist groups provide ideological fuel and often direct support for terrorist activities. They aim to impose their strict interpretation of Islam through violence, targeting the state, minorities, and even those within the majority who do not adhere to their views. The TTP, for example, seeks to establish its version of Sharia law through violent means. As per an unconfirmed assessment there are approximate 55,000 madrasas in Pakistan today which act as a nursery for this jihadist ideology.[38] A complete takeover by these terrorist organizations something like what happened in Afghanistan or Syria seems to be a difficult preposition however in a scenario of fragmented Pakistan they can wield adequate power and influence to dictate a format of governance that is fundamentalist in character which in itself would be dangerous.

- Plausibility of a fragmented Pakistan is debatable but cannot be overruled. This would be the most dangerous preposition for Pakistan given the threat to very identity and sovereignty of the state. A singular factor like economy, internal disturbance, a violent religious renaissance or involvement of an even external force cannot lead to fragmentation of Pakistan in a classic sense. However given the very character of Pakistan, the vulnerabilities of various institutions and propensity of fault lines to manifest in a dangerous proportion, combination of various factors leading to total anarchy in the state cannot be negated. A fragmented Pakistan is a possibility in a similar way as Bangladesh became a reality. The end state of this scenario would therefore translate into 'Balkanised Demise' of Jinnah's Pakistan which failed to live the dream.

Question of the most Plausible Scenario

Having discussed the various scenarios, the most important question is what could be the most plausible scenario for the future of Pakistan given the changing character of global environment. It is not an easy debate definitely. The world is becoming increasingly unpredictable today transiting from a unipolar (US dominated) or bipolar (US-Soviet) system toward multi-polarity. Emerging powers like China, India, Brazil and regional entities such as Turkey and Iran are asserting more influence. Power is more diffused – not only among states but also among non-state actors (corporations, NGOs and cyber actors). There's growing US-China rivalry over trade, tech, geo-politics and leadership. Institutions like the UN, WTO World Bank, and IMF are facing legitimacy challenges. Rising nationalism, populism, and authoritarianism has weakened the liberal internationalist model. Rules-based systems are being contested by power-based approaches. Tech dominance (AI, 5G, quantum computing etc.) is driving the geopolitical competition. Basically, there is a shift from a hegemonic leader role of US to a more balancing role in a contested order. In such a situation, it is unpredictable whether the global powers, the Islamic Umaa or even the international institutions would be in a position to rescue Pakistan under duress of various fault lines.

A functional Pakistan is not in favour of India or the region at large. I am aware it sounds alarmist but let me elaborate. Pakistan's true character is revisionist. It is neither contended with what it received in partition nor with what it could achieve subsequently in the 78 years of its history. As Christine Fair notes, Pakistan is rarely content with the status quo, especially in its regional security posture – often seeking strategic depth, revisionist outcomes in Kashmir, and influence in Afghanistan to tilt the balance in its favour.[39] Separation of East Pakistan shattered the shallow pride of an artificial nation defeating the adopted idea of a Muslim nationhood. However, Pakistan never accepted the truth. For several decades now Pakistan has tried to keep the idea alive mainly because there is no other alternate. Pakistan has also not come to terms with the fact that demonstration of animosity against India cannot make up for all the other deficiencies in functioning of the state. Whether it is on the basis of religion or the feeling that India has snatched from Pakistan what it deserved, the hatred for India across all sections of the society is a national characteristic which would never change. It for these reasons that a functional Pakistan with robust and powerful state institutions is detrimental to the overall security and stability of India and region at large.

A fragile Pakistan where the state is on the brink of anarchy is an intriguing scenario. It is a situation where the institutions and establishment are weak although not completely redundant. The fault lines would deteriorate but would not implode remaining well within manageable parameters. This would be a scenario wherein compliance to a desired behaviour could be achieved without a threat to the neighbourhood and the extended region. In order to achieve the same all factors impacting conduct of the state have to be managed in a manner so that any form of erratic behaviour could be obviated. Sustaining a fragile Pakistan would be a difficult preposition. Pakistan is expected to leverage its primary strengths to include geo-strategic bargain, the Muslim card and the nuclear bogey to extract every pound of flesh. In no situation would the Military or even the main polity like to be seen as the culprit or blameworthy for driving Pakistan into such a situation. Apropos, maintenance of a fragile Pakistan would warrant a deft global diplomacy and a well thought through engagement from the neighbourhood to achieve desired deterrence against Pakistan.

A fragmented Pakistan would be a mixed bag for India and the region. Pakistan does not have an appetite for another Bangladesh (in the form of Baluchistan, Pashtunistan, Sindhudesh or even Gilgit-Blatistan). If that happens it would definitely be a scenario of civil war either self- inflicted or triggered by the powerful Army. Nonetheless, I would like to suggest that a limited balkanization of Pakistan would be an advantage distinctly for India. It would crush the head of Pakistan to an extent that it remains weak and submissive for a reasonable future. It is obvious that such a situation would be attributed to India much before it implodes and in probability Pakistan Army would make an attempt to deflect the focus by raising the ante against India. However, within the construct of the regional and the global environment that has been painted for debating this scenario (India rising-world dismissive), the probability of any such adventure by Pakistan especially when there is a boiling pot of secession at their hands is limited if not impossible. While I accord highest feasibility of such a scenario to emerge, it is also prudent to ponder whether a nation can really split or Balkanize. History is replete with events wherein widening faultlines along political, social and ethnic differences have eventually led to fragmentation of a state. After the Allied victory in World War II, Yugoslavia was set up as a federation of six republics with borders drawn along ethnic and historical lines. However, when Tito died and communism fell, these republics pulled apart leading to breakup of Yugoslavia.[40] The reasons for disintegration ranged from cultural and religious divides between the ethnic groups, memories of WW-II atrocities committed by all sides and impact of centrifugal nationalist forces. In the case of USSR, besides several other reasons it was Gorbachev's decision to allow elections with a multi-party system and create a presidency for the Soviet Union which eventually destabilized Communist control and led to the collapse of Soviet Union.[41] All these instances establish that decay and deterioration of political, military and civilian institutions coupled with mass protests and unrest can in fact lead to disintegration of the country.

Conclusion

I have endeavoured to draw out certain relevant scenarios accentuated by deepening of existential fault lines in Pakistan within an assessed global and regional environment. Whether these scenarios would unfold or not as we move into the next decade, I would leave that decision with the readers. In order to define a strategic framework for India to engage with Pakistan in the coming 10-15 years, I would be carrying forward the best and the worst case scenario for Pakistan in the next Chapter for a pragmatic analysis of the fault lines.

Notes

1 Stephen P Cohen, 2011, "The Future of Pakistan and Others", pp 82, Brookings Institution Press.

2 Bank for International Settlements. Annual Economic Report 2025. June 30, 2025. https://www.bis.org/publ/arpdf/ar2025e.htm.

3 United Nations, World Population Prospects 2022, Medium fertility variant, July 2022.

4 William Milam, 2011, Essay in "The Future of Pakistan", edited by Stephen P. Cohen and Barnett R. Rubin, Brookings Institution Press, p 57.

5 Stephen M. Walt, 2018, "The Hell of Good Intentions: America's Foreign Policy Elite and the Decline of U.S. Primacy", Farrar, Straus and Giroux.

6 "Promoting Chinese Priorities and the China Model", https://www.cfr.org/china-global-governance.

7 "China's rise and its implications for International Relations and Northeast Asia", https://www.sciencedirect.com/science/article.

8 World Bank, Global Economic Prospects, January 2025, press release, January 16, 2025; World Bank, "Global economy to expand by 2.7% in 2025, 2026," aa.com.tr, January 17, 2025.

9 International Monetary Fund, "Friend shoring Could Have Some Not So Friendly Downsides," Investopedia, 2023.

10 "Climate Catastrophe," n.d., https://www.climateemergencyinstitute.com/refugees.

11 National Intelligence Council, Global Trends 2040: A More Contested World, Washington, DC: Office of the Director of National Intelligence, March 2021, https://www.dni.gov/files/ODNI/documents/assessments/GlobalTrends_2040.pdf.

12 Guardian Staff Reporter, "Pakistan Summons US Envoy Over Joe Biden's 'Most Dangerous Nation' Remark," The Guardian, October 15, 2022, https://www.theguardian.com/world/2022/oct/15/pakistan-summons-us-envoy-over-joe-bidens-most-dangerous-nation-remark.

13 Institute for Economics & Peace, Global Terrorism Index 2025, Vision of Humanity, March 6, 2025.

14 Ibid.

15 Associated Press, "Pakistan to deport over 1.3 million undocumented Afghan refugees; slow rollout in Khyber Pakhtunkhwa", April 15, 2025.

16 Ayesha Siddiqa, "Pakistan's Counterterrorism Gamble", Carnegie Endowment for International Peace, July 10, 2014. https://carnegieendowment.org/2014/07/10/pakistan-s-counterterrorism-gamble-pub-56279.

17 Farhan Bokhari, "Pakistan's Long Bailout History with the IMF," Financial Times, March 2023.

18 NDTV News Desk, "Huge Protests in Pak After Imran Khan&Amp;#039;S Arrest, Supporters Storm Army HQ," NDTV, May 10, 2023, https://www.ndtv.com/world-news/protesters-enter-pak-army-headquarters-after-imran-khans-arrest-report-4019411.

19 Reuters, "Pakistan amends law to extend powerful army chief's service tenure," November 4, 2024.

20 National Electric Power Regulatory Authority, "State of the Industry Report 2023–24", Islamabad: NEPRA, January 2025.

21 Ember, "Pakistan | Ember," April 11, 2025, https://ember-energy.org/countries-and-regions/pakistan.

22 Times of India, "Pakistan cuts 150,000 jobs, dissolves 6 ministries for $7 billion IMF deal," Sept 29, 2024.

23 Adeel Khan, "The Rise of PTI: Populism, Social Media and Civil-Military Politics in Pakistan," Asian Survey 62, no. 4 (July/August 2022): 652–675

24 Ayesha Jalal, 1990, "The State of Martial Rule: The Origins of Pakistan's Political Economy of Defence", Cambridge University Press.

25 Akbar S. Ahmed, 1986, "Pakistan Society: Islam, Ethnicity and Leadership in South Asia", Oxford University Press, Karachi.

26 Reuters, "Pakistan floods '10th costliest disaster' in a decade," Dawn, November 17, 2022.

27 Human Rights Watch, "Pakistan: Military Clampdown Tarnishes Elections," February 6, 2024, https://www.hrw.org/news/2024/02/06/pakistan-military-clampdown-tarnishes-elections.

28 Ayaz Gul, "Taliban Rejects Pakistan's Fencing of Afghan Border," Voice of America, January 3, 2022, https://www.voanews.com/a/taliban-rejects-pakistan-s-fencing-of-afghan-border/6381257.html.

29 Ap, "Pakistan and Iran Agree to Work Together to Improve Security After Tit-for-tat Airstrikes," The Hindu, January 29, 2024, https://www.thehindu.com/news/international/pakistan-and-iran-agree-to-work-together-to-improve-security-after-tit-for-tat-airstrikes/

30 World Bank, International Debt Report 2024, reporting external debt at $130.85 billion; Fitch Ratings, "Pakistan faces big external financing risks despite economic progress," Reuters, February 7, 2025.

31 World Bank, Pakistan Floods 2022: Post-Disaster Needs Assessment (PDNA), October 2022, https://documents.worldbank.org/en/publication/documents-reports/documentdetail/099735010272230663/pakistan-floods-2022-post-disaster-needs-assessment.

32 A "Lebanonized state" refers to a country that has descended into a condition of deep internal fragmentation, sectarian conflict, weak governance, and loss of central authority, often marked by the presence of powerful non-state actors or militias that rival or overpower the official state apparatus.

33 Ayesha Siddiqa, 2007, "Military Inc.: Inside Pakistan's Military Economy", London: Pluto Press.

34 Fareed Zakaria, 2008, "The Post-American World", W.W. Norton & Company.
35 International Crisis Group, Pakistan's Risky Border Calculus: Eastern Brinkmanship and Western Volatility, Asia Report No. 329, March 2024.

36 Financial Times, "Pakistan's banks enjoy soaring profits on interest from mounting government debt", Financial Times, July 31, 2024.

37 Ayesha Jalal, 2014, "The Struggle for Pakistan: A Muslim Homeland and Global Politics", (Cambridge, MA: Harvard University Press.

38 Farhan Hanif Siddiqi, 2009, "Madrasas and Militancy in Pakistan: Internal and External Dynamics," Contemporary South Asia.

39 C. Christine Fair, 2014, "Fighting to the End: The Pakistan Army's Way of War", New York: Oxford University Press.

40 Misha Glenny, 1804-1999, "The Balkans: Nationalism, War and the Great Powers", New York: Viking, 2000.

41 Archie Brown, 1996, "The Gorbachev Factor", Oxford: Oxford University Press.

Chapter Six

Implications of Fault Lines and Resultant Scenarios for India

> *"In 1972 at Shimla, India chose to bet on an optimistic outlook on Pakistan. At the end of the day, it resulted in both a revanchist Pakistan and a continuing problem in Jammu & Kashmir. That it has taken us so long to link talks with Pakistan to cessation of terrorism speaks for itself."*
>
> —Dr S. Jaishankar[1]

India cannot remain insular to what happens in Pakistan when there are so many threads that connect the two nations, historically as well as culturally. In the previous chapters we have tried to define the character of Pakistan as a state and the key infirmities which impacts its future. But how critically does all that influence India's own growth and security in the region, is an important question. The terrorist strikes in Uri, Pulwama and recently in Pahalgam have elicited a strong response from India each time defining new thresholds and dynamics. This has demonstrated a trend of perpetual friction between the two Asian neighbours which cannot be overlooked. Apropos, it is important to study the impact of identified fault lines and likely scenarios in Pakistan from India's perspective so as to draw out relevant inferences.

Can India Marginalize Pakistan?

What happens in Pakistan has a cascading impact on its neighbourhood. It is not only because of the fact that demography on either side of border is congruent but also due to common challenges of security, resources and climate. India and Pakistan are as much alike as they are different. India and Pakistan were cut from the same piece of cloth after securing independence from the

British. We inherited similar systems and models of governance as established by the British. We understand each other's language and culture which influences our behaviour. India's Muslim population is second highest in the world.[2] But that's where the similarities seize. India and Pakistan after independence chose different trajectories which today has established India as a responsible and progressive nation while Pakistan is still stuck with ideological dilemmas, crippling institutions and stumbling economy.

Pakistan has been a state in constant denial. It did not accept the partition in entirety and has been struggling with this reality ever since. Instead of consolidating the national institutions and building the country, Pakistan spent its initial years in nugatory debates of state and religion. The fact that it assassinated its first Prime Minister and took almost nine years to adopt its constitution reflects the chaos and uncertainty of initial years.[3] Pakistan has always blamed India for an unfair partition, proclaiming India's desire to see Pakistan as a failed idea. The creators of Pakistan were well aware that idea of a Muslim nation was a good political gimmick to consolidate Muslim voices before India's independence but was it adequate to create a separate nation was always doubtful. Pakistan, as we have seen, is much divided at several levels than united by a singular thread of religion. The establishment in Pakistan is conscious of this infirmity and hence created a systemic narrative of anti-Indianness ingrained deeply in the DNA of the society. There is a deep sense of insecurity across all sections of the society in Pakistan that India is determined to see Pakistan fail and has always cherished the idea of integrating Pakistan back into its folds which is so distant from reality. Creation of Bangladesh only reinforced this false narrative, demonstrated by the fact that Pakistan Army was so conveniently absolved of all its wrongdoing in East Pakistan, shifting the complete blame on an allegedly expansionist India. It is for this reason of inherent and deep-rooted hatred against India that Pakistan has to be treated with suspicion and mistrust.

Another facet of constant consternation between India and Pakistan is its obsession with Kashmir. Kashmir has no longer remained a matter of dispute for Pakistan but has emerged more as a symbol of national identity and cause. Pakistan's obsession with Kashmir stems from a combination of historical claims, ideological beliefs, and strategic interests. Since the partition of British India in 1947, Pakistan has viewed Kashmir – India's only Muslim-majority state – as an unfinished part of two-nation theory.[4] This belief has driven its persistent political, diplomatic and sometimes military efforts to challenge India's sovereignty over the region. Pakistan has made Kashmir central to its foreign policy, often raising the issue in international forums and providing support to separatist movements and terrorist groups operating in the area. This single-minded focus has come at a cost, diverting its resources and attention from internal development and governance. It has resulted in four wars with India (including 1971 war) which have turned out almost counter-productive for Pakistan.[5] Despite changing global attitudes and India's firm stance that Kashmir is an internal matter, Pakistan continues to view the issue as a core national cause, deeply embedded in its civil-military narrative and national psyche. Strategy to pursue proxy war in J&K is indicative of a toxic mindset which is not likely to change.

Another important factor which necessitates that India pays adequate and continuous attention to Pakistan is the institution of military in Pakistan that fails to change. From Yahya Khan to Zia-ul-Haq and Musharraf to now Asim Munir, Pakistani Generals have often carried their belligerence towards India on their sleeve, looking to leverage the animosity for strengthening own position. By emphasizing the 'Indian threat', Pakistan Army has been able to justify its outsized role in governance, budget allocations and national security policy.[6] Whether it was the folly of founding fathers or incompetence of successive generation of politicians, Pakistan's military has succeeded in amassing disproportionate strength, securing a position on the highest pedestal. Such has been the extent of manipulation by Pakistan Army and the ideological bankruptcy perpetrated by it, that today military authority has become almost unquestionable in Pakistan. It is no secret that Pakistan's military draws its major strength by manipulating a self-created threat from India, which has allowed it to apportion largest share in the budget and finances of the country. Leaders like Zia-ul-Haq have infused the India-Pakistan contest with religious overtones, depicting it as a struggle between Muslim Pakistan and Hindu India. This resonates with segments of the population and strengthens the moral authority of Army. For Pakistan's Army, belligerence and conflict with India is an existential necessity for which it would be ready to go to any length. It would therefore be in the interest of India to keep a watchful eye on Pakistan besides continuously investing in military capabilities to retain decisive edge against the western adversary.

Pakistan's lethal romance with fundamentalist groups and Islamic terrorist organizations also makes it imperative that India keeps its guard up to prevent any percolation of the problem across the border. Initially used as tools of strategic depth in Afghanistan and leverage in Kashmir, these groups eventually turned inward, unleashing a wave of extremism and violence within Pakistan itself. Attacks on civilians, security forces, and minority communities have destabilized regions like Khyber Pakhtunkhwa and Baluchistan, undermining national security and eroding public trust in the state's ability to maintain order. Internationally, Pakistan's reputation has suffered greatly; it has faced sanctions, diplomatic isolation, and inclusion on the Financial Action Task Force (FATF) grey list, damaging foreign investment and economic prospects.[7] Furthermore, the empowerment of militant ideologies has contributed to radicalization of society, weakened democratic institutions, and hindered the country's progress. In trying to use terrorism as a strategic tool, Pakistan has created a monster that threatens its own stability and global standing. India is not insulated from religious indoctrination. Vulnerability of Indian Muslims to fundamentalism and violence cannot be overruled. India in its interest therefore must monitor the implosion of Islamic terrorist organizations in Pakistan while maintaining a close watch on domestic front.

Pakistan has always tried to externalize its problems which stems from a mix of historical events, geopolitical scenario and impact of foreign and domestic policies. Instead of addressing systemic issues such as corruption, weak governance, radicalization and economic mismanagement, successive Pakistani governments and the powerful military establishment have often used the perceived threat from India to divert public attention and foster national unity. This externalization has been a key tool in justifying military dominance in politics, excessive defence spending and the curtailment of civil liberties. Internationally, Pakistan has frequently portrayed itself as a victim of external manipulation, while downplaying its own role in fostering extremism and cross-border terrorism. This narrative has hindered Pakistan's credibility on the global stage, leaving the country trapped in a cycle of denial and underdevelopment. Off late Pakistan has been portraying itself as a victim of terrorism as it grapples with a rapidly deteriorating internal security situation. However, it does not admit that the devil has been created by Pakistan itself who tried to cash upon the opportunities emerging from complex geo-strategic games played out in the region, ending up burning their own hand in the bargain. With an extremely vitiated internal environment today, Pakistan finds itself yet again on the brink of a catastrophe. Its tendency to always shift blame to India, or to deflect the internal turmoil to Kashmir necessitates that India keeps a close watch on Pakistan. Any attempt by Pakistan Army to play up India must be repelled with an iron hand to retain a deterrence against misadventure.

Destiny of India and Pakistan is intertwined. A contentious history marked by multiple wars, border disputes and persistent cross-border terrorism defines the complexity of relationship between the two nuclear powers of South Asia. Pakistan's alleged support for terrorist groups targeting India, coupled with its singular military orientation, poses a significant security threat. Additionally, Pakistan's unstable political and economic situation could exacerbate regional instability, potentially spilling over into India. The complex interplay of all these issues, alongside Pakistan's strategic alignment with China, heightens India's need for vigilance to safeguard its national interests and regional stability.

Fault Lines from India's Prism

In the third chapter I have discussed the existential fault lines in Pakistan and how they play an important role in shaping the destiny of the state. Before we identify the strategic contours of India's engagement with Pakistan, it is important to understand the impact of these fault lines on India. India's fate is intertwined with Pakistan and that is a brute reality. Whether Pakistan progresses to become a stable state or spirals into chaos, India cannot remain insulated to the developments across its western borders. It is partly attributable to the shared history which has been scarred by mutual distrust but largely due to the fact that Pakistan continues to associate its relevance by demonstrating a character which is anti-India. Anti-India in the sense of religion, unjust partition, intent of keeping Pakistan straddled or sometimes extrapolated to extent of absurdity by claiming India's strategy to see a further fragmented Pakistan. For this reason and many, it is imperative that Pakistan's fault lines are analysed from the prism of India to draw correct inferences.

Identity is the most critical of Pakistan's fault lines and has common threads connected with India. The 'Two-Nation Theory' which argued that Hindus and Muslims were distinct nations and incapable of coexisting peacefully within a single state has driven the narrative of Pakistan's identity. This foundational premise inherently frames India as 'the other' which allegedly pose an existential threat to Pakistan's existence. Heavily intertwined with its Islamic character, Pakistan has often promoted an agenda that India (with its Hindu majority) is adversarial to Muslim identity.[8] The influence of religious conservatism in Pakistan, sometimes aligning with extremist ideologies, has further strained the relationship between the two countries. Even the Kashmir dispute is viewed through a religious lens, linked to Pakistan's national and religious identity. Some analysts suggest that this contributes to the perception of Pakistan as a destabilizing force rooted in religious extremism. As a consequence of this flawed narrative, Pakistan continues to portray India as an 'eternal enemy' and profess itself as a 'strong security state'.[9] For India it is a direct threat to security and stability as Pakistan exploits its identity as a basis for their belligerent actions against India.

The Pakistani military has historically played a significant role in shaping the national narrative, often using anti-India sentiment to rally domestic support and deflect criticism. Pakistan's internal struggles such as Pashtun nationalism, Baloch insurgency, and resentment over Punjabi dominance, challenges its identity as the protector of Islam. These internal divisions have the potential of imploding which can destabilize security in the region. Pakistan's identity has often been constructed around opposition to India, with military doctrines and foreign policy emphasizing strategic competition. The presence of terrorist groups operating from Pakistani territory, perpetrating cross-border terrorism has exacerbated tensions between India and Pakistan. Furthermore, the fact that Pakistan is a nuclear state which resorts to nuclear sabre rattling and jingoism at the slightest of nudge, is an apparent threat to the security and growth of India. Overall Pakistan's adoption of an adversarial identity against India is a potent threat which has to be duly factored in the overall security calculus in the region.

Religion and ideology are as much a binding factor as a fault line in Pakistan.[10] It can be an enabler if Pakistan manages to address the basic expectations of the society which includes economic progress, security and adequate opportunities for business or employment. But in a state which has failed to adopt a long term strategy to strengthen the economy and has politicized Islam to consolidate power, religion and ideology would continue to remain a factor of instability instead of aggregating national effort. From India's perspective, this ideological positioning can be treated as a threat when it fosters extremism, promotes radical nationalism and supports anti-India sentiments in policy as well as society. This bankruptcy of faith and manipulation of ideological viewpoint creates friction fostering a confrontational relation with India.

Religious extremism and ideological radicalization in Pakistan have given rise to terrorist groups like LeT and JeM, who have been directly involved in various terrorist incidents in India over the years to include 2001 Indian Parliament attack, 2008 Mumbai attacks, 2019 Pulwama bombing and the recent targeting of tourists in Pahalgam in Apr 2025. These groups have thrived and operated in Pakistan with impunity creating an asymmetrical threat to India. Internally, the sectarian and religious divide within Pakistan to include Sunni-Shia tensions, persecution of Ahmadiyyas and attack on minorities have been a catalyst of internal instability and disorder.[11] Communal narrative in Pakistan sometimes find echo in India as well which can lend to ideological polarization. This can not only strain the Hindu-Muslim relations within India but also affect the secular fabric of Indian society. The religious and ideological divisions within Pakistan are not just domestic issues but have tangible cross-border implications. For instance, Deobandi-inspired groups like TTP, share ideological affinity with anti-national outfits in India like Indian Mujahedeen, which exacerbates radicalization in the border states and Muslim majority areas.

Pakistan's ideological framing as a defender of Muslim interests in South Asia underpins its nuclear doctrine, which explicitly targets India. The notion of 'strategic parity' with India, driven by ideological rivalry, has led to an arms race, including development of tactical nuclear weapons.[12] This escalates risks for India, as any conventional conflict can spiral into a nuclear crisis. Pakistan has been flaunting its irrational strategy of nuclear use of weapons to create uncertainty and derive concessions. India has been calling out the bluff of Pakistan in this regard but that has not diminished the anxiety and concern of global community which feels that levers in Pakistan would not be coerced to refrain from use of nuclear weapons in a scenario of probable setback in any conflict. Another consequence of Pakistan's obsession with India is its inability to provide effective governance in the state due to prioritization of ideological goals over economic development, fosters lawlessness and lack of development. Pakistan's ideological rhetoric, amplified by disinformation can stoke communal tensions in India, particularly among its Muslim population which remains extremely vulnerable to religious influence and propaganda. Religious and ideological fault lines in Pakistan can strain India's social fabric fuelling a narrative of hostility and religious intolerance thereby marginalizing moderate voices.

Ethnic fault lines in Pakistan especially among Baloch, Sindhis, Pashtuns, Punjabis and Muhajirs have several indirect and direct implications for India. These internal fractures and divisions affect Pakistan's stability, which in turn can influence regional dynamics and India's strategic environment. Ethnic unrest in Baluchistan and Khyber Pakhtunkhwa has stretched the security forces beyond comfort leading to significant casualties both to civilians as well as military.[13] With spate in violence, armed groups like TTP and BLA has challenged the credibility of Pakistan Army, placing them in the dock of public scrutiny. Islamabad has repeatedly blamed India for providing financial support to the secessionists and Iran for allowing them safe hideouts. India has officially maintained that these allegations don't merit any serious consideration and that Pakistan must introspect its own support to terrorism. In the year 2024 Pakistan lost almost 358 security personnel in almost 521 terrorist incidents which places a question mark on the professional conduct of operations by Pakistan security forces.[14] While Pakistan's pre-engagement with its internal challenges may be in India's favour to some extent, the possibility of Pakistan Army shifting the focus back to India to divert attention of its own domestic population is extremely plausible so as to prevent further damage to Pakistan Army's reputation. A bruised Pakistan bogged down by internal conflicts and an overwhelming law and order situation would be more unpredictable and potentially more desperate. The recent terrorist attack in Pahalgam resulting in a short India-Pakistan skirmish may be interpreted as a manifestation of a similar attempt.

The existence of ethnic insurgencies in Pakistan often provides a narrative for the Pakistani military and intelligence establishment to maintain their dominant role in the country's politics and security apparatus. They can present themselves as the sole guarantors of Pakistan's unity, often by emphasizing external threats. Ethnic discontent can also fuel the growth of extremist organizations thriving in Pakistan who can extend their operational sphere across the border. Although this seems to be less probable, yet it cannot be negated completely. The ethnic fault line involving the Pashtun population divided across Durand Line affects Pakistan's long term strategy on Afghanistan. It is often debated whether a volatile western Pakistan would be detrimental to India's interest in Afghanistan.[15] India has been attempting to resume a frozen dialogue with Taliban which is yet to witness a complete fructification. Should India treat the current freeze in Pakistan-Afghanistan relations as an opportunity? Absolutely yes. But would it deliver the required dividends, is something which only future would tell. Pakistan's internal challenges present strategic opportunities for India; however, the extent to which India should desire Pakistan to remain embroiled in its own crises is a complex dilemma that requires careful and long-term strategic assessment. In essence, the ethnic fault lines in Pakistan contribute to a pervasive sense of instability and mistrust against India. While India officially maintains a policy of non-interference in Pakistan's internal affairs, the consequences of these fault lines, particularly in terms of cross-border security and regional stability, directly impact India's strategic interests and security calculations.

It is beyond debate that Military is the strongest institution in Pakistan. Its raison d'etre is concentrated in a fabricated threat from India which has allowed Pakistan Army to amass enormous power in the country. It is for this reason that any threat to its status would elicit strongest intervention from Pakistan Army. Whenever Pakistan has been in turmoil, the most convenient excuse has been to export the blame to India or incite hollow fervour of nationalism driven by a narrative of Islam under danger. Pakistan Army is not only a military institution but an establishment which has spread its tentacles in every discipline of governance and public life. Originally established to support the welfare of military personnel and their families, the Pakistan Army's economic ventures have evolved into sprawling business enterprises. The recent $3.3 billion green energy project in the Cholistan Desert, undertaken by the military, underscores the expanding economic interests and influence of the armed forces in Pakistan's commercial landscape.[16] Pakistan Army has historically played a dominant role in foreign affairs and diplomatic engagements of the country, far beyond its constitutionally defined mandate. The military controls government's policies related to relationship with global players and neighbouring countries especially China, India and Afghanistan by leveraging security of the country. Over the years, Pakistan Army has made itself indispensable in a manner that has led to immense concentration of power in the institution. This is indeed unprecedented and merits due acknowledgement.

Influence of Pakistan Army in the matters of the state is irrefutable. But can Pakistan Army bring together the complete nation during contingency or crisis is debatable. The Army has always championed itself as a professional force par excellence claiming victory in all wars fought with India (although it lost East Pakistan in 1971). It was the sword arm of western powers during Soviet-Afghan War, training mujahideens from across the world. During GWOT, Pakistan was a frontline state providing much needed logistic support to the US and its coalition partners in Afghanistan.[17] All that aside, Pakistan Army does have some significant challenges and shortcomings which raises concerns about its credibility. Army's long history of interfering in politics has polarized public opinion. There have been increasing incidents of soldiers especially in Frontier Corps refusing to participate in operations directed against TTP.[18] Some soldiers reportedly feel that they are being placed in high-risk missions without adequate logistical support or clear mission. In 2024, Pakistan's security forces experienced their highest casualty rates in nearly a decade, with an average of approximately seven fatalities per day (both military and civilians). There is a rising discontentment amongst young officers against the senior leadership and their decisions. At the higher level, manipulation for selfish interest and power is rampant which adversely impacts the ethos of the institution. Today, Pakistan Army is under duress, which seriously accentuates the irrationality in its behaviour. From India's point of view, any dent to Pakistan Army's image amidst its domestic population is a matter of concern. A military under pressure at home may seek to externalize problems such as provoking tension with India or Afghanistan to rally domestic support or divert attention from internal failures. It could create space for terrorist groups, making them more autonomous or emboldened. Either of the situation would be detrimental to India's interest and therefore must be handled appropriately.

Terrorism is one of Pakistan's most critical fault lines, deeply affecting its internal stability and regional dynamics. The resurgence of terrorism in Khyber

Pakhtunkhwa, Baluchistan and even urban centres like Karachi has created widespread fear and instability. Many of these terrorist groups, once considered 'strategic assets', have turned against the state, leading to blowback in the form of insurgency and terrorism. For India, this fault line presents a complex challenge with security, diplomatic and strategic consequences. Historically, Pakistan based terror groups like LeT, JeM and others have been involved in attacks on Indian soil, including high-profile incidents like the 2008 Mumbai attacks, 2019 Pulwama bombing and 2025 Pahalgam massacre.[19] If such groups grow stronger, the frequency and intensity of cross-border terrorism could increase, particularly in sensitive regions like J&K. A more radicalized environment in Pakistan might lead to terrorists acquiring more sophisticated weapons and training, potentially making future attacks deadlier and harder to prevent. The spread of radical ideologies also fuels anti-India sentiment within Pakistan, making diplomatic engagement more difficult and encouraging a hostile public narrative. Radicalization in Pakistan can inspire sympathizers within India (though a limited possibility) which could threaten internal peace and communal harmony. An unstable Pakistan with empowered extremist factions may also pose a threat to security of nuclear assets, raising global concerns.

The assumption that rising terrorism in Pakistan will primarily harm India oversimplifies the regional dynamic. While India faces clear risks, Pakistan's own fragility to include economic collapse, internal unrest and military strain means it would suffer more, potentially limiting its ability to sustain proxy wars. However, the skirmish between India and Pakistan in 2025 after Pahalgam attack demonstrates rapid escalation triggered by terrorist incidents. Rise in terrorism and radical groups in Pakistan would heighten India's security challenges, undermining its developmental objectives. It would strain diplomacy, escalate regional tensions and burden India's resources, while China's growing influence could complicate the equation. India must balance robust counterterrorism with diplomatic efforts to tackle Pakistan, in order to prevent a volatile neighbour from becoming a regional tinderbox.

Growth of Pakistan-based radical groups could unsettle Afghanistan, where TTP already operates, creating a broader arc of instability. While the Taliban may not support all of them openly, their inability or unwillingness to control these factions gives these groups space to grow and operate across both borders.

This would further weaken Kabul's fragile control, undermining regional peace efforts, turning the Afghanistan-Pakistan border into a permanent theatre of extremism and insurgency. India's $3 billion investment in Afghanistan's infrastructure would also be at risk.[20] India has invested heavily in infrastructure, education, healthcare and connectivity projects, including the Salma Dam, Zaranj-Delaram highway and the Parliament building in Kabul. Resurgence of terrorist groups like the Islamic State-Khorasan Province (ISKP) and the continued presence of Pakistan-backed radical outfits in Afghanistan compromises the security and stability necessary for these projects to operate and sustain. India has made an outreach to Taliban but the interplay between the terrorist groups thriving in Pakistan and forces controlling Afghanistan would continue to impact the security dynamics in the region. To summarize, rise of terrorism in Pakistan directly undermines India's security, strains bilateral relations and increases the risk of military escalation. It is a challenge that requires sustained vigilance, intelligence cooperation and strategic diplomacy.

Pakistan, like many developing countries, has a large youth population, often referred to as a 'youth bulge' or 'demographic dividend'. A demographic dividend occurs when a country's working-age population (typically 15 to 60 years old) grows significantly larger than its dependent population (children and elderly). If this large workforce is healthy, educated and employed, it can be a powerful engine for economic growth and development. However, if a country fails to capitalize on this demographic dividend, it can turn into a 'demographic disaster' or 'demographic burden'. This means a large number of unemployed or underemployed youth leads to social, economic and political instability. Pakistan's inability to effectively harness its demographic dividend would not only impede its own grown and affect stability but would also have a negative impact on India. Pakistan is a country which breeds on Islamic sentiment. Over a period of time, the society in Pakistan has become increasingly tolerant to Islamic discourse and proliferation of radical thought process. Mushrooming of madrassas across the state especially in Punjab is testimony of the growing trend. For many poor families, especially in rural areas, madrassas offer free education, meals and lodging, filling a critical gap left by underfunded public schools. Significant number of madrassas have been linked to sectarianism or extremism, particularly those receiving foreign funding (e.g. from Saudi Arabia or Iran) with specific ideological agendas.

Presence of a vast number of uneducated, unskilled and unemployed youth becomes a fertile ground for these radical entities who lure them with a false sense of identity and financial incentives. Another development on Pakistan's extremism scene has been the rise of the so called 'educated Jihadists'. Some recent incidents of violence have been attributed to graduates from Pakistan's mainstream educational institutions, especially universities, who belong to the more affluent middle and upper middle classes.[21] This trend is indicative of a very conservative pattern with radical characteristics which is proliferating amongst the youth in a 'latent' and 'passive' manner.

Pakistan has been home to terror outfits of various kinds, divided into several categories based on their ideological orientation, socio-political identity and economic objectives. Paradoxically not only have these terrorist groups established their primary bases in Pakistan but they also receive active or passive assistance from the agencies entrenched within the security establishment of Pakistan.[22] Even after Pakistan's post-9/11 partnership with the US, several Islamist groups continue to enjoy close ties with the State with popularity among certain sections of the public. Deobandi Ulema of the Jamiat Ulema Islam (JUI) participates in electoral politics while describing Jihad as a sacred right and obligation.[23] These narrative appeal to the audience in madrassas and unemployed youth who fall easy prey to extremism. Pakistan does not seem to possess the capacity as well as the will to eradicate terrorism, as it is constrained by the influence enjoyed by the various terrorist groups in complicity with Army and ISI. Pakistan would continue to be a hot bed of Islamic extremism as long as the operative terrorist organizations resort to violence in the name of Islam and the public keeps showcasing acceptance to this phenomenon. The terrorist groups, which draw inspiration from the religious groups in Pakistan have developed into Frankenstein's monsters for both people and the state, coupled with selective approach of security agencies towards counter-terrorism, which makes 'Peace in Pakistan' or mellowing down of 'Pakistan sponsored terrorism' in its neighbourhood a distant dream. Unemployed and frustrated youth are fodder for operatives of this strategy which not only destabilizes the region but also generate an El Nino effect over India, exacerbating existing security challenges. Pakistan's inability to engage its youth is not only a domestic issue but a grave concern with direct and indirect repercussions for India's security.

A worsening water crisis is a major fault line impacting social order and stability in Pakistan. As a lower riparian country, Pakistan relies heavily on the Indus River system, whose major tributaries originate in India. Water scarcity, driven by population growth, climate change, poor water management and depleting groundwater, has intensified Pakistan's dependence on these shared rivers. The Indus River system, vital for both Pakistan and India has emerged as a major flashpoint in recent years. India's stance on placing the Indus Waters Treaty (IWT) in abeyance poses significant challenge for Pakistan, particularly in terms of water security, agriculture, and regional stability. As a largely agrarian economy, Pakistan depends heavily on the western rivers. Disruption in water flow from India, either through dam construction or flow manipulation, can severely affect Pakistan, leading to food insecurity and economic strain. Suspension of IWT post the Pahalgam attacks in 2025 has been vehemently rejected by Pakistan which called India's unilateral decision as 'illegal', 'unjust' and an 'act of water warfare'. Pakistan has indicated plans to raise the issue in various international forums, including the World Bank (which facilitated the treaty), the Permanent Court of Arbitration, and the International Court of Justice. Water restrictions add a dangerous dimension to already fragile relationship between India and Pakistan. For Pakistan, this stance not only threatens its environmental and economic stability but also triggers an urgent diplomatic and strategic response to safeguard its national interests.

Pakistan's water crisis is driven by a combination of factors, including climate change, overuse of resources and poor management of water systems. Pakistan's water availability per capita has dropped by over 70% in the past 70 years, currently standing at just 1,017 cubic meters, well below the global water scarcity threshold of 1,000 cubic meters.[24] This alarming decline is compounded by the fact that Pakistan's water storage capacity is only enough to cover 30 days of demand, far lower than the global average of 120 days. The catastrophic floods of 2022, which displaced over 33 million people and submerged a third of the country, serve as a stark reminder of the consequences of poor water management and inadequate climate resilience in Pakistan.[25] A severe water crisis in Pakistan could destabilize its economy and society, potentially fuelling extremism or anti-India sentiment. This could increase cross-border terrorism, which India has cited as a reason for reconsidering the IWT. Heightened tensions might also lead to military posturing, diverting resources and attention from domestic priorities in both countries.

Implications of Various Scenarios

Having looked at Pakistan's fault lines from India's perspective, it is pertinent to debate the implications of various scenarios that may emerge in Pakistan as identified in the previous chapter. The metaphor, 'One can choose friends but not the neighbours', best defines the existential reality of India-Pakistan relations. With a shared land border of approximately 3,323 kilometers and an overlapping maritime zone, India cannot afford to remain indifferent to developments within Pakistan.[26] It is a fact of history that the circumstances in which Pakistan was created and the course it decided to take thereafter has brought in an element of perennial apprehension between the two neighbours. Pakistan's own journey has been marred by political uncertainty and military dominance. Today, anti-India sentiment has formed a part of Pakistan's DNA. Apropos, whatever may be the status of Pakistan in the future, India would have to be prepared to uphold its national interest while averting Pakistan from playing spoilsport in India's pursuit for regional and global ascendency.

Functional Pakistan: A Worst Case Scenario for India

Behaviour of a functional Pakistan or a status defined closest to stability has to be audited from the perspective of key drivers that define the state. Having understood the character of Pakistan it is safe to assume that stability in Pakistan hinges on four factors which are strategic relevance, economy, military and society. I have intentionally excluded political stability from the above as this is an institution which has got completely subsumed into military over time. Since many decades now, military and its leadership has accomplished complete dominance over politics, resulting in absolute defanging of political class. Whether it was Liaquat Ali Khan, The Bhuttos, Sharifs or even Imran Khan, stature of a national political figure could not withstand the onslaught of an ostentatious and powerful military. Pakistan Army has seized power whenever they felt the institution was in threat, making the political class a convenient scapegoat. While Pakistan Army championed its position secured on the high pedestal, the political parties never made an endeavour to win the confidence of the masses who remained sceptical of their intentions. As a consequence, Pakistan got a dysfunctional polity in blessing which has often worked as a puppet in the hands of the military.

Amongst all factors, strategic relevance carries maximum weightage. For

Pakistan to acquire a functional status, it would be safe to assume that it has succeeded in leveraging its strategic advantage to remain relevant to the global powers. China for one has invested heavily in the idea called Pakistan. It desires access to the Arabic seas and major Sea Lines of Communication emanating from Europe which Pakistan provides for. The jostle for relevance in Asia is quite evident as witnessed during the recent developments post Pahalgam terrorist attack, the ongoing power play in Bangladesh-Myanmar and obviously the Taiwan crisis. Every important player to include US, China, EU, S Arabia or even Turkey remains invested in the region impacting the overall strategic disposition in the region. A stable Pakistan entails active engagement of all stakeholders who would not allow a crisis to implode Pakistan. A stable Pakistan would also necessitate a functional economy operating at an optimum level. Pakistan as such does not have the required ingredients to achieve the same without the assistance of the global financial institutions and its friends in need. Whether it is IMF, World Bank or the guiding angels of Pakistan, financial assistance would not come through till such time Pakistan commits to toe the line and comply with regulations. This is infact a tall order given the level of manipulation perpetrated by the ruling class and obviously the military establishment in serving their own interests. Economic comfort therefore implies that the elite would feel restrained while military may comply reluctantly which jeopardises the longevity of balance and stability altogether.

Coming to the other factors of military and society, both have a complex relationship premised on manipulation and unquestionable faith. In a functional Pakistan one thing is certain that military would be in a most comfortable position both externally and internally. For several decades military in Pakistan has drawn its strength and power by externalizing its pivot so that it can deflect the attention of the society from real problems. It has thrived on the narrative of 'Islam in danger' and 'India is a perpetual enemy' for so many years that every time the institution feels it is losing credibility; it plays the combined anti India and religion card to galvanize public opinion in its favour. A functional Pakistan implies that Pakistan's military has been successful in cementing its status as saviour of Pakistan while establishing parity with India militarily. A strong military in Pakistan would be against the interest of India and a greater concern for Indian armed forces. Besides the factors already discussed, Pakistan's society remains the most complex vector whose complete manifestation has not yet been witnessed. Pakistan's early years were characterised by a strong feudalistic system which has today metamorphosed into a complex web of social disparity, orthodoxy, unemployment and bitterness. The society had always been conscious religiously but the recent decades has witnessed a more rabid and radical practice of the same which threatens to endanger the very core of social order and stability. In true sense, Pakistan's society is a tinderbox today. When we talk of a stable Pakistan, it is assumed that the vulnerabilities of a volatile society have been managed well which indicates superimposition of stronger factor. This could be military or coercion of an external agency/stakeholder which itself raises an alarm for India.

So, while we have tried to hypothecate a scenario of a functional Pakistan, few striking characteristics of this state emerge distinctly. Foremost amongst that would be Pakistan making itself indispensable strategically while its economy rides an upswing. The military is pitched at a most comfortable position bestowed with power, influence and stature. The society which today appears to be on the verge of implosion has somehow stabilized and is no longer a footstone straddling Pakistan's development. This is a state which is most dangerous and alarming for India. Pakistan is endemically anti-Indian which no amount of goodwill or outreach can alter. Its very existence is based on the idea that India is hazardous for Muslims. The notion of a stable Pakistan being beneficial for India is a mirage. While some argue that a stable, prosperous Pakistan would inherently lead to a more peaceful neighbourhood, others contend that Pakistan's foundational ideology and historical baggage makes such a scenario unlikely to bring genuine benefits. Apropos, a functional Pakistan translates into a strong Pakistan which with its perennial antagonism for India would be even more dangerous necessitating India to commit resources and energy to acquire commensurate leverages.

Fragile Pakistan: An Uncertain Scenario for India

A fragile Pakistan is a state defined by marked deterioration of its inherent fault lines, each threatening to disbalance Pakistan significantly. It is however debatable whether a single fault line is capable of putting Pakistan off balance or would that require combined implosion of more than one crisis. In the recent years, especially after the pandemic we have witnessed Pakistan at its lowest ebb. Pakistan faced its worst economic crisis in many years with inflation spiralling out of control. Having been placed on FATF grey list, its access to financial aid from donors and financial institutions also got restricted with international pressure mounting to demonstrate accountable behaviour. As per a realistic assessment, Pakistan suffered cumulative real GDP losses of approximately US $38 billion between 2008 and 2019 alone.[27] Beyond the direct financial losses, grey listing had severe reputational consequences, signalling to the international community that Pakistan has deficiencies in its anti-money laundering and counter-terrorism financing regimes. This led to strain in Pakistan's relationship with international partners and isolation from global financial systems. On the domestic front, Pakistan is facing one of its worst internal security situation with a mounting crisis in Baluchistan and an unrelenting TTP. The politico-military engagement is transitioning through a sensitive phase with a fragile understanding in pace, while Imran Khan remains in custody on frivolous grounds. It was a common assessment of the strategic fraternity that an extremely fragile Pakistan constrained by a multitude of problems as discussed above would impose the required deterrence on the state and the establishment conducive to India's concerns. But with the execution of Pahalgam terrorist attack resulting in a short skirmish between the two nuclear neighbours, Pakistan has thrown the deterrence theory out of the window, demonstrating the intent and capability of leveraging the anti-India card to draw the attention of its domestic audience away from the crises at home.

A deeper perspective on Pakistan's behaviour brings out important insights. One thing that emerges distinctly, not only after the Pahalgam incident but even from events that happened in the past is the unbridled and unquestionable power that is wielded by Pakistan military in every aspect of state function and decision making. Pakistan military lead by the Army is and has been the most powerful institution in the state which can even lead a nation to the brink of a war disregarding domestic or global concerns. This is nothing but autocracy and brute control in its truest sense. Therefore, whatever may be the approach adopted by India in tackling Pakistan, its military has to be duly factored in every aspect. The second most important derivative of considered examination is the fact that anti-India sentiment in the backdrop of religious incongruity is the basic characteristic of Pakistan's society which may get suppressed from time to time but would always remain potent in engagement between the two nations. Every time Pakistan is in crisis, it is this animosity against India, so called land of kafirs, which is played up to stoke nationalist sentiment and draw the attention away from trouble at home. These two factors, of an all-powerful Army and the idea of Pakistan rooted in anti-Indianness is the real centre of gravity in Pakistan from which the establishment draws its actual strength. As far as Pakistan's foreign policy is considered, it has always taken recourse in being a client state, offering lucrative dividends to interested customers. Its longstanding alliance with China is driven by economic needs and strategic counterbalancing against India. Meanwhile, its relationship with the US has oscillated between cooperation and mistrust, shaped by security imperatives and regional interests. With other stakeholders as well Pakistan has not altered its approach. A situation of fragility in Pakistan thus is bound to elicit appropriate concern and intervention from the strategic clienteles which must be acknowledged and factored by India in drawing its strategy against Pakistan.

When we talk about a fragile scenario in Pakistan, it must be acknowledged that it is a status which would force a strong reaction from Pakistan. Pakistan has always attempted to externalize its problems seeking global intervention and domestic deflection. A Pakistan embroiled in its own problems is definitely in India's interest, but to what extent these pressures would continue to favour India is something which needs to be analysed correctly. From a historical perspective, the period when Pakistan was probably in its weakest state was during the 1971 war with India leading to liberation of East Pakistan. For a country like Pakistan, to be dismembered is not only a failure of its sovereignty but also places a question mark on the very idea of its creation. But even at that moment, one institution which was never cast under suspicion was Pakistan military who deflected the complete blame on an allegedly expansionist India and a weak polity at home. Pakistan Army not only manipulated the domestic narrative in its favour but also insulated itself from any criticism for the atrocities committed in East Pakistan in the aftermath of political unrest. This resilience of Pakistan's establishment to evade scrutiny and accountability during crisis is an important aspect which has to be duly factored while strategizing against a fragile Pakistan.

It must be acknowledged that Pakistan is an irrational state which has repeatedly demonstrated unpredictable behaviour especially in its engagement with India. Whether it was the Kargil incursions in 1999 or the numerous terrorist attacks perpetrated in Indian territory starting from Parliament attack in 2001, Pakistan has always kept a dagger hidden under its cloak under the false pretext of improving relations. Pakistan's lower-threshold rhetoric regarding the use of tactical nuclear weapons in response to conventional military operations by India is another example of unpredictable and irrational behaviour under duress. India for one has to be extremely wary of this propensity and not get carried away with the belief in tolerance and congenial coexistence especially in case with Pakistan. A feeble or weak Pakistan which is irrational at the same time is expected to do the unexpected with or without patronage of its well-wishers. The assumption that a constrained or weak Pakistan straddled with myriads of challenges would deter it from attempting any misadventure against India has been debunked recently after Pakistan decided to up the ante with Pahalgam terrorist attack. India has embarked on a consolidated diplomatic, economic and strategic outreach to strangulate Pakistan and hold it accountable for perpetrating terrorism in India but it is quite apparent that same has not been effective as India would have desired. It is thus important for India to understand that pushing Pakistan to the wall when it is at its most feeble state would entail collateral cost for which India would have to be well prepared.

Fragmented Pakistan: A Preferred Scenario for India

From an adversarial point of view, fragmented Pakistan would generate a much-hyped euphoria and gratification in India which is but obvious. However, when we talk about disintegration of a state it has to be viewed with utmost scepticism as it would have far reaching implications for the state and the region at large. Pakistan has suffered the experience once before. It lost its eastern wing in 1971, which constituted a significant portion of its landmass and population. This immediately reduced Pakistan's geographical size and eliminated its non-contiguous nature. The very basis of Pakistan's existence, the Two-Nation Theory, which asserted that Muslims of the subcontinent constituted a single nation distinct from Hindus was severely undermined. The fact that a Muslim majority region seceded on linguistic and cultural grounds, rather than religious ones, dealt a blow to Pakistan's foundational ideology. However, the recent speeches by the current COAS of Pakistan Army, General Asim Munir indicates towards revival of the same ideology amidst lack of an agenda for mobilizing larger public opinion. The loss has led to a profound sense of national trauma and resentment, which has impacted Pakistan's strategic thinking and its relationship with India ever since. While discussing this scenario, I would not go into the plausibility of disintegration of Pakistan as a consequence of singular fault line or a combination of more than one as the same has been deliberated in adequate detail in previous chapters. What would be more prudent is to interpret the aftermath of such an event in real terms and the resultant impact on India to be specific.

A fragmented Pakistan implies breaking away of those regions which have proclaimed secessionist aspirations. Fault lines challenging the sovereignty of Pakistan exist in Baluchistan, KPK, Sindh and to some extent in Gilgit-Baltistan besides Saraiki belt of Punjab. However, Baluchistan is the only movement which has some credence to challenge the writ and control of the central authority. Why do I say that? Pashtunistan – a proposed independent state for the Pashtun people, primarily living in Pakistan's KPK and parts of Afghanistan has historical and political significance, but its contemporary weightage is limited and nuanced. The warlords in Pashtun belt want restoration of conditions that existed before FATA was dissolved and merged to form KPK in 2018. Their larger aspiration is linked to de-recognition of Durand line that physically severed the Pashtun nation. Pashtuns, who share a common language, culture, history and tribal affiliations, found themselves arbitrarily divided between two different states. This division separated families, tribes and communities that had historically moved and interacted freely across these artificial borders for centuries. Amongst Pashtuns, the sentiment of cultural and historical contiguity is more important that seeking secession from Pakistan. In this melee, TTP has a totally different agenda which is not constrained to a secessionist idea. In case of Sindh the movement is not that strong enough and exists only as a political ideology. For this fault line to accentuate in a manner that it acquires the dimension of a secessionist movement is significantly limited. Gilgit-Baltistan and Saraiki fault line is limited to greater political and provincial autonomy. Gilgit-Baltistan is a complex discourse with intertwined threads of sectarianism, political neglect and parity with other provinces. Muffled voices for re-integration with India which gets traction from time to time does not have enough weight to challenge the central authority. Similarly, Saraiki movement is focused on recognition based on linguistic identity. The people residing in the Saraiki belt seek division of Punjab province to cater for the aspiration of Saraiki belt. Overall, in a scenario of fragmented Pakistan only Baluchistan and to some extent Pashtunistan has adequate weightage to create conditions for disintegration of Pakistan.

In case of both Baluchistan and Pashtunistan, India would not have to face the challenge of immediate repercussion as these provinces do not share a land border with India. The larger concern for India would be to refute accusations of supporting these movements which Pakistan would leverage aggressively. The ongoing fifth insurgency in Baluchistan has acquired violent proportion. Besides Pakistani security forces facing serious reverses and mounting casualties, the armed groups have also targeted non-locals (mostly Punjabis) causing widespread panic and fear. The inability of Pakistan military to contain the violence has dented its image amongst masses threatening to endanger its credibility. As an excuse for the reverses faced in so called anti-terrorist operations, Pakistan Army and its establishment has often taken recourse in blaming India for providing tacit support to secessionist groups like BLA and BRF. The fact that Baluchistan constitutes around 6% of the total population of Pakistan occupying a landmass of almost 40% gives a feeling that the secessionist movement lacks weight.[28] But the ground situation is different. The sensational attacks undertaken by Baloch fighters has shaken up the country fuelling fear of Baluchistan's secession. Similarly, action by TTP and affiliated Pashtun groups in KPK has also challenged the authority of Pakistani security forces but in a comparatively reduced proportion. Fragmentation of Pakistan would not come through in a jolt. It would follow the course of increasing defiance, human rights violations, probably a civil war and a protracted period of contestation for establishing control. India through this process would be faced with multi-faceted challenges to include expectation of moral and material support, calling out the human rights violations and finally the dilemma of recognizing the new dispensation. Overall, India would have to tread with caution adopting a nuanced and well thought out approach in managing its relationship with a fragmented Pakistan. It would be preposterous to assume that a disintegrated Pakistan would alter its behaviour towards India drastically. The character of Pakistan has been to blame its belligerents for own follies, sometimes to an extent with dangerous proportion. India's strategy would have to be aligned to this reality. Such a situation wherein two provinces of Pakistan are embroiled in secessionist unrest, would have an impact on the overall security situation in the region. Presence of religious actors (they are no longer non-state actors) in abundance would further complicate the security paradigm in Indo-Pakistan region highly susceptible to extension in the complete region. Apropos, a fragmented Pakistan would weaken the state exponentially but, in all probability, would also plunge the region into a state of extreme turmoil and unrest. For this situation and everything else, India has no choice but to be prepared extremely well.

World View on Future Scenarios

The world looks at Pakistan with varied interests. In the eventuality of a fragmented Pakistan, the US and the West would want that the strategic dividend of the region is retained, while engaging with the fragmented components. The nuclear status of Pakistan and the safety of nuclear arsenal as well as infrastructure would be a major concern. Chinese would definitely prefer a united Pakistan owing to the massive investments that they have made in the country. Today, Pakistan Army is one of the largest importers of Chinese military hardware.[29] China would therefore wish that Pakistan Army retains its influence in the national affairs even in a fragmented configuration. As also a stronger Pakistan is definitely a more effective counter to India which is rising in stature in the region. The OIC countries are likely to display inhibitions but would settle for four members instead of one as they have very limited role in all the three scenarios discussed above. Afghanistan and Iran, would be more comfortable dealing with smaller neighbours. The sovereignty of a Pashtunistan and Baluchistan would however be a persistent bone of contention for common ethnic regions in Pakistan, Iran and Afghanistan. Russia and the Central Asian Republics would see no major change in their outlook towards the region and would likely align with the changed scenario. Overall, the world would look at evolving scenarios in Pakistan with skepticism looking to secure their strategic and national interest which would always remain paramount and enduring.

Conclusion

In this chapter I have endeavoured to contextualise the manifestation of various fault lines and resultant scenarios in Pakistan to draw relevant implications for India. In today's world of uncertainty and flux hypothecation of future has become extremely difficult. Geo-politics is transcending a new paradigm wherein rule based world order is rapidly collapsing to secure national interests even at the cost of ideology, culture and beliefs. The unpredictability of global response to any crisis has enhanced significantly, placing a question mark on the expected behaviour of any state. It is therefore pertinent for India to closely monitor the manifestation of various fault lines in Pakistan and be prepared to respond to any scenario that may emerge in the neighbourhood. Like I said before, the past, present and future of India and Pakistan is so intertwined that neither can ignore the other. It would be boisterous of India to think that Pakistan has become increasingly irrelevant, as India rises in its stature as a regional and global power. Pakistan is an envious neighbour who would not rest to see the rise of India without playing spoilsport. It is in India's interest to dominate the escalatory ladder in India-Pakistan relations to safeguard its national interests at every cost. In the next and final chapter, I would attempt to define the strategic framework for India in its engagement with Pakistan to ensure unfolding of the preferred scenario in Pakistan over a time period of next 10-15 years.

Notes

1 Press Trust of India and Business Standard, "Simla Agreement Resulted in 'revanchist' Pakistan, Problems in J-K: Jaishankar," Www.Business-Standard.Com, November 14, 2019, https://www.business-standard.com

2 Press Trust of India, "India Home to Second Largest Population of Muslims in World: President Murmu," www.ndtv.com, July 12, 2023, https://www.ndtv.com

3 Ian Talbot,2009, "Pakistan: A Modern History",Hurst & Co.

4 Tariq Aqil, "Kashmir: Unfinished Agenda of the Partition," Pakistan Observer, June 2, 2025.

5 Sushant Sareen, "Pakistan's Strategic Miscalculations: Lessons from 1947 to Kargil," Observer Research Foundation, February 2020.

6 Lt Gen Prakash Katoch, "Pakistan's National Security Policy," Indian Defence Review, September 2, 2024, https://indiandefencereview.com/pakistans-national-security-policy/

7 FATF, "Jurisdictions under Increased Monitoring – Pakistan," Financial Action Task Force, June 2022, https://www.fatf-gafi.org/en/countries/pakistan.html

8 Yelena Biberman, "How Pakistan's Army Fuels Islamic Extremism," Foreign Policy,

October 18, 2019, https://foreignpolicy.com/2019/10/18/pakistan-army-islamic-extremism-kashmir-india-hindutva/

9 Muhammed Aamir Raza, 2023, "Pakistan's Security Doctrine: The Dissection", Centre for Research and Security Studies.

10 Husain Haqqani, 2005, "Pakistan: Between Mosque and Military", Carnegie Endowment for International Peace.

11 Ayesha Siddiqa, 2020, "Pakistan's Minorities and the State," South Asia: Journal of South Asian Studies 43, no. 4.

12 Amey Velangi & Kartik Bommakanti, "Pakistan's Tactical Nuclear Weapons Limit India's Conventional Military Options," ORF Expert Speak, June 25, 2024.

13 Al Jazeera, "Dozens of Soldiers, Fighters Killed in Baloch Separatist Attack in Pakistan," *Al Jazeera*, February 1, 2025, https://www.aljazeera.com/news.

14 Pak Institute for Peace Studies (PIPS), "Pakistan Security Report 2024: An Abridged Version," January 15, 2025, https://www.pakpips.com

15 Shanthie Mariet D'Souza, "India's Stakes in Afghanistan: Maintaining Engagement in Uncertain Times," Institute of South Asian Studies, ISAS Working Paper No. 381

16 Agencies, "Ambitious Project Launched to Turn Cholistan Green," dawn.com, February 16, 2025, https://www.dawn.com/news/1892222.

17 Lubna Sunawar, "Pakistan as a Frontline State in War Against Terrorism: Cost & Benefit Analysis", Pakistan Research Database, n.d., https://www.prdb.pk/article/pakistan-as-a-frontline-state-in-war-against-terrorism-cost-1896.

18 "DFAT Country Information Report Pakistan", 30 April 2025, https://www.dfat.gov.au/sites/default/files/country-information-report-pakistan.pdf.

19 Ajai Sahni, "Lashkar-e-Taiba: Past Operations and Organizational Profile," South Asia Terrorism Portal, 2023. https://www.satp.org

20 Reuters. "Taliban Says India is 'Significant Regional Partner' after Meeting." Reuters, January 9, 2025. https://www.reuters.com/world/asia-pacific/taliban-say-india-is-significant-regional-partner-after-meeting-2025-01-09/.

21 Madeeha Anwar, "Pakistan's Emerging Threat: Highly Educated Youth Gravitate to Radicalization," VOA News, May 6, 2017.

22 Pakistan Army and Terrorism; An unholy alliance. (n.d.). https://www.efsas.org/publications/study-papers/pakistan-army-and-terrorism

23 Abou Zahab, Mariam and Olivier Roy, 2004, " Islamist Networks: The Afghan-Pakistan Connection", Columbia University Press.

24 NS Manhas, 2025, "Pakistan's growing water crisis: A future in jeopardy", India Today, https://www.indiatoday.in/opinion/story/pakistan-growing-water-crisis-a-future-in-jeopardy.

25 United Nations Office for the Coordination of Humanitarian Affairs (UNOCHA), Pakistan Floods 2022: Humanitarian Response Plan, September 2022, https://reliefweb.int/report/pakistan/pakistan-floods-2022-humanitarian-response-plan-revised-version-september-2022.

26 "Ministry of Home Affairs | Government of India," n.d., https://www.mha.gov.in/en/divisionofmha/border-management-i-division#

27 Government of Pakistan, Ministry of Finance, Economic Survey of Pakistan 2019–20,

Chapter 6: Security Situation and Its Impact, Islamabad, 2020, https://www.finance.gov.pk/survey_1920.html.

28 International Crisis Group, Pakistan: The Worsening Conflict in Baluchistan, Asia Report No. 119, September 2006. https://www.crisisgroup.org/asia/south-asia/pakistan/pakistan-worsening-conflict-balochistan.

29 Stockholm International Peace Research Institute (SIPRI), Trends in International Arms Transfers, 2023, March 2024, https://sipri.org/publications/2024/sipri-fact-sheets/trends-in-international-arms-transfers-2023.

Chapter Seven

Recommended Strategies for India

> "*India's best approach is not war, but smart statecraft – isolating Pakistan diplomatically, raising the cost of terror, and investing in internal resilience.*"
>
> —Ashley Tillis[1]

Fragmented Pakistan: A Fait Accompli

Pakistan has always nurtured a deep-rooted adversarial attitude towards India and irrespective of the scenarios, the belligerence is not likely to go away. 'Hate India' is a survival kit in Pakistan. Pakistan feels a jugular connect with Kashmir which it considers to be an unfinished agenda. Pakistan has been a practitioner of terrorism as a state policy which it would continue to profess and orchestrate not only in Kashmir but rest of India as well. Pahalgam terrorist attack is a livid demonstration of toxic belligerence harboured by Pakistan for India. This also emanates from a perennial need for seeking relevance in the geo-strategic paradigm where Pakistan feels its importance is rapidly diminishing. The nuclear weapons and their security in Pakistan is also a major regional challenge. Pakistan would continue its nuclear sabre rattling to offset convention asymmetry with Indian Armed Forces. Besides increasing Sino-Pakistan ties, threat of military collusivity and binary impact on the Western and Northern borders are important considerations which cannot be overlooked. Apropos, a subjugated and fragmented Pakistan is the most preferred scenario which serves the best interest of India.

While India is rising, a struggling and simmering Pakistan is in its best interest. Pursuit for a fragmented Pakistan over a period of next 10-15 years is ambitious. However, a concerted approach towards it must commence in a concerted manner to realize the intended objective in a realistic time frame.

From the perspective of academic objectivity, the desired end state for Pakistan can be qualified in short term (2035-40) and long term (2045-50) as under:

Fragmented Pakistan (2035-40)	Balkanized Pakistan (2045-50)
• **Autonomous Baluchistan**: Complete loss of Pakistan's central control proclaimed independence by Baluchistan • **KPK**: Restive with greater allegiance to Afghanistan-Pak forced to cede political space • **Sindh**: Co-equal power sharing with Punjab, demands of separation • **POJK/GB**: Major simmering and resultant repression and alienation; Increased demands to break away/join India; Protest against presence/control of PLA	• **Baluchistan**: Global and regional recognition • **KPK**: Restive extension of Afghanistan into Pakistan • **Sindh**: Economically stable Sindhudesh. • **POJK/GB** - POJK and GB merger with India – Long awaited aim achieved • **Pakistan** reduced to Punjabistan – Troubles with India contained

Source: Jinnah's Pakistan - A forgotten tale

Strategic Construct

Having identified the fault-lines within Pakistan, the options for India is to either wait for ultimate balkanization of Pakistan or to catalyse the process by utilising resources at disposal in all domains. The lines of operation as nation to achieve the desired end state has to be multi-dimensional but converging. Important tenets of the 'whole of nation approach' required to achieve the same, are listed below:

- **A Shrewd and Engaging Diplomacy**. This may not necessarily be restricted to diplomatic engagement on a bilateral level, but may have to find traction at a wider canvas on a regional and global level. The simple aim of this tenet should be to paint Pakistan as a pariah nation and isolate it globally as much as desired. India's rising stature as a global entity of consequence must be leveraged to shape global opinion on Pakistan. Besides engaging the diplomatic corps, intellectuals and technocrats from academia and industry also need to be engaged in this effort. India's approach to diplomatically isolate Pakistan has to adapt to changing geopolitical dynamics and shifting currents in international relations. India would also have to consistently raise the issue of state-sponsored terrorism originating from Pakistan at international forums like the UN, FATF and other multilateral organizations. The goal is to build a global consensus that Pakistan is a terror state which is reluctant to take demonstrable action against extremist groups operating from its soil. India's overall diplomatic effort has to be premised on naming and shaming, imposing costs, strengthening alliances and demonstrating credible deterrence, all while navigating the complexities of a nuclearized neighbourhood.

- **An Overbearing and Dictating Economy**. India must make all endeavours to boost the economy on a regional and global level. China needs to be engaged economically more pro-actively to decouple it from Pakistan to the maximum extent possible. The already crumbling economy of Pakistan must and should be so strangled that it emerges as the most critical faultline triggering disgruntlement and disenchantment amongst the people of Pakistan against the dysfunctional system. India's economic stature can be leveraged to exert pressure on social media houses – the likes of Twitter, Instagram and Facebook to drive own narrative. Pakistan's economy is often reliant on loans and bailouts from international financial institutions. India, as a significant global economy and a member of these institutions, can leverage its influence to argue against lenient bailouts or loans to Pakistan on the pretext that funds are unscrupulously diverted to fuel the state-sponsored terrorism industry. Suspension of Indus Water Treaty and trade with Pakistan, like it was done post Pahalgam incident in 2025, are tools for holding Pakistani establishment accountable while demonstrating India's resolve and low threshold for belligerent actions by Pakistan.
- **Measured and Precise Perception Management**. Much has been spoken and written about impact of perception management in an India-Pakistan construct. The IW architecture entails selection of themes, identifying the target population predominately fence sitters and targeting the same with carefully curated, personalised themes based on location, position and work profile of the target. The aim is to rally common masses towards anarchy, discredit government and military as also create law and order situation with demands for transition. While a lot has already been done in IW domain, there is a felt need to have unity of effort, a coherent roadmap for future and

a focussed implementation plan. The IW framework is required to be established at Strategic, Theatre and Regional levels to achieve realistic dividends.

- **Menacing Military Prowess.** In Pakistan while all the other tenets including polity, diplomacy, and economy may have failed, the instrument of National Power that has continued to uphold the image as steadfast 'Saviour of Pakistan' is the military. Pakistan' identity and stature is associated with military therefore to elicit desirable behaviour and conduct from Pakistan would necessitate that this instrument is dominated and subdued at all costs. In light of undeterred military modernisation of Pakistan, India's own military transformation, absorption of technology and integration of niche technologies to include drone capability, IW, cyber, Precision Munitions, infrastructure-development etc. must advance on full throttle till such time decisive edge is gained over Pakistan. The aim should be to exponentially widen existing numerical and technical asymmetries in all domain while retaining conventional superiority over Pakistan. The consideration of counterbalancing collusive threat from China and to some extent now with a rapidly belligerent Bangladesh would also need to be factored in the long term perspective planning and military modernization of Indian Armed Forces.
- **Leveraging Intelligence.** The elite intelligence agency of the nation (R&AW) must be empowered to further strengthen its capabilities in all domains to deliver the required dividends whenever a situation demands so. It has to have tangible assets across the world, proactive in tailoring events rather responding to contingencies. The recent trend of neutralization of criminals and extremists in Pakistan may be the handiwork of anybody, but own intelligence agencies must and should leverage such options with disdain and finesse, cost notwithstanding. Such efforts would further accentuate the deep-rooted mistrust amongst various factions of the society in Pakistan thereby worsening already deep fault-lines in the state. Cultivation off fifth columnists, disgruntled military soldiers the likes of Adil Raza, social media influencers and youth icons to push desired narratives behind enemy lines can cause disgruntlement among the common populace, weaken

civil administration and cause disinformation which can catalyse Balkanisation.

Preparing the Grounds

To enable India to achieve the desired end state in all the future scenarios, it is essential that the ground for future plans are prepared in advance. As highlighted by Robert Greens in his book 'The 33 Strategies of War',[2] it is important to undermine the enemy before hitting him. This is known as the 'Perfect Economy Strategy' as per which endeavour is made to weaken the adversary through a series of concurrent and successive maneuvers. In doing so, it is important that the potency of Pakistan is degraded in all domains. India must make a strong case to exert international pressure on Pakistan to acknowledge state's role in harbouring terrorist groups which has become a potent threat to the overall security in the region. Involvement of extremist organizations and groups in Kashmir, Bangladesh and now even in Nigeria (with reports confirming their involvement in training of Boko Haram), has authenticated Pakistan's state policy of leveraging these hybrids groups as strategic levers for own interest. In order to discredit Pakistan's proxy strategy and dismantle the terrorist infrastructure, the threat of financial blacklisting must be reactivated to again include Pakistan in the FATF Grey/Black list. The military-politics imbalance in Pakistan has to be called out. India must vociferously support the democratic process by exposing the evil nexus between Pakistan Army and fringe political groups. The current economic situation should be exploited by pressurizing Pakistan to curtail military spending and preventing it from apportioning aid money towards funding of these terrorist groups. India must raise voice at all appropriate forums to call out the human rights violations and atrocities committed by Pakistan Army in Baluchistan and other affected provinces while standing firmly in solidarity with the long standing aspirations of people of this region. The illegal occupation of PoJK and GB should also be given the required traction while concurrently investing on people-to-people engagements based on shared cultural ties. Water is a huge lever which can provide significant dividends. The IWT was kept in abeyance after the Pahalgam incident which has established a new normal in India's perceived response doctrine. Such steps and more are thus necessary to strangulate Pakistan from all directions while preparing grounds for a favourable scenario for India.

Diplomatic Informational Military Economic (DIME) Stranglehold

In order to accomplish intended fragmentation of Pakistan, the various ethno-linguistic-religious fault lines of all provinces should be approached through tailor made design crafted across the complete DIME architecture. While some measures of the complete DIME paradigm would be applicable in planning strategies for every province, more emphasis would have to be laid on a specific factor for each province to derive desired effect and result:

- **Diplomacy – Baluchistan**. Highlighting the plight of ethnic minorities in Baluchistan from the ramparts of Red Fort in the Independence Day speech of PM on 15 Aug 2016 is a classic manifestation of diplomacy to support the cause. There is also a need to provide suitable platform to expat Balochs to highlight the atrocities and the injustice meted out to the people of Baluchistan by Pakistan Army and their Government. India would have to device a diplomatic approach which is neither seen as complaint with the Baluchistan freedom struggle nor indifferent to the aspirations of Balochs who yearn for support of the regional and global community. Baluchistan is an opportunity for India which has to be handled with extreme dexterity. It is indeed a test of India's diplomatic wisdom in meeting the expectations of own national interest while upholding the principle of non-interference and objectivity.
- **Information – KPK**. Information domain including the various social media platforms can be judiciously exploited to orchestrate a campaign highlighting neglect and alienation of the people of KPK to the international community. The ethnic linkage of KPK with Afghanistan could be highlighted which would further consolidate the demands for greater Pashtunistan. IW is an important tool for perception management and has the potential to be a game changer in shaping the overall opinion of domestic as well as international audience in accordance with the identified national objectives.
- **Military – PoJK/GB**. A multi-pronged approach steered by a strong military intent has to be developed to achieve physical and psychological integration of PoJK/GB. It would entail augmentation of defence infrastructure to sustain operations, developing required

military capabilities and capacities besides synergizing military efforts across multiple domains to accomplish a decisive victory. Transformation of the armed forces aligned to the changing character of war and based on integration of new concepts and emerging technologies is an essential imperative to accomplish absolute integration of PoJK/GB in future. Simultaneous action in other domains also must continue to achieve support of the people of PoJK and GB to combat the threat of collusivity.

- **Economy – Sindh**. Sindh shares strong historical and ethnic linkage with India where numerous economic activities were undertaken between the people in the not so distant a past. Integration of Sindh through application of economic instrument is the most viable approach which can deliver assured dividends. At the same time regional efforts like calling for grey-listing of Pakistan (FATF), imposition of economic restrictions and sanctions besides requirement to wean away China off their blind investments in Pakistan, are certain other aspects which have to be leveraged.

Lines of Effort

As highlighted in the approach above, concerted efforts in the respective DIME verticals would further accentuate the fault lines and compound the challenges of Pakistan thereby causing it to cave in and pave the way towards its possible fragmentation and subsequent Balkanization. To ensure that Pakistan's future contours are drawn in a manner which suits India, requisite instruments have to be leveraged across all domains. This 'Whole of Nation' effort would necessitate actions at different levels covered under the following heads:

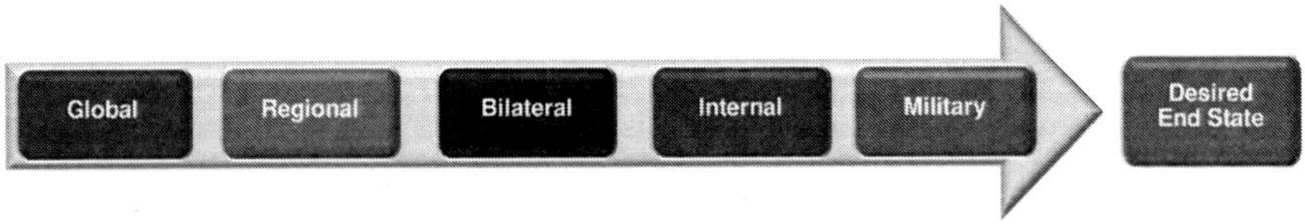

- **Global**
  - ✓ **Drying up Guardian Angels.**
    - The world is becoming increasingly self-centric with rule based world order coming under considerable stress. In such times, the need of the hour is a strong diplomatic engagement with

the US, Russia, EU and OIC countries – thus disincentivizing ambivalence towards Pakistan. This should be a sustained effort as part of a strong and focused foreign policy formulated in due course.

- It is important to repeatedly highlight the dubiousity of Pakistan's legality on J&K, Baluchistan and KPK. India must re-emphasize this critical aspect of Pakistan's identity in suitable platforms with due fairness and conviction.
- India must bring out the fallacious conduct of Pakistan in the GWOT wherein it put up a façade of an important collaborator for western forces while discreetly providing shelter and safe haven to Osama Bin Laden in the backyard of Pakistan Army's Cantonment. Pakistan's real character of being the epicenter of terrorism must be emphatically reiterated to the global community.
- Portray India's secular and inclusive growth and at the same time expose Pakistan's ill treatment of minorities, thereby highlighting the ethnic conflicts and fault-lines.
- India must flex its economic muscle to leverage the influencer guilds in G7 nations to hold Pakistan accountable. India's active role in global bodies and economic forums has already created the right atmosphere to highlight this issue in correct perspective.
- India must understand that weaning away international support for Pakistan in global forums is a multifaceted and delicate diplomatic endeavor that requires a strategic approach rooted in evidence and sustained engagement.

✓ **Befriend Pakistan's Friends.**

- Pakistan to be projected in every forum as the epicenter of terrorism.
- Highlight Pakistan as a liability to all stakeholders (especially China and Islamic countries).
- Balochi connect with both Oman and Iran to be promoted.

- Clear the mist over the treatment of minorities within India which has been an irritant in relations of India with the Islamic world.
- Engagement with Turkey and certain central Asian countries has to be reflected from the perspective of their recent behavior post Pahalgam incident. Although desirable to develop leverages which can act as deterrent against overt support of these countries for Pakistan in crisis and otherwise, India's engagement has to be measured and realistic without compromising on core values and interests.

✓ **Economic Strangulation.**

- Leverage India's influence over the World Bank and IMF in crafting conditional bailouts for Pakistan with due accountability.
- Put in sustained efforts to get Pakistan placed back on the FATF grey/black list as it would have a major impact on its economy.
- India must make an endeavor to dry up foreign direct investment (FDI) in Pakistan. This would be much difficult than understood otherwise. India could strategically highlight Pakistan's economic vulnerabilities, such as its high external debt, limited foreign exchange reserves, and political instability to discourage FDI and deter multinational corporations from investing in Pakistan.
- While direct bilateral trade between the two nations is already minimal due to strained relations and various restrictions, including India's revocation of Pakistan's Most Favoured Nation (MFN) status and imposition of high tariffs, unofficial trade through third countries remains substantial. India must focus on intensifying efforts to curb this informal trade, which is estimated to be billions of dollars annually.
- Bringing military spending under scrutiny of global financial bodies by linking it to release of subsequent aid and credits.

- **Regional.**
  - ✓ **Getting the Flock Together.**
    - Getting the flock together in South Asia is of utmost importance. India has not done very well in this domain. To consolidate regional opinion in its favour and to hold Pakistan accountable, India would have to break the perceived mould of big brother and perception of indifference shared by the Asian neighbours.
    - Indian rupee needs to become the preferred currency in the region. This can be a key strategic objective for India, aiming to reduce dependence on the US Dollar, enhance regional economic integration and bolster India's geopolitical influence.
    - India needs to give the right impetus to South Asian Free Trade Agreement. Progress on the agreement has been significantly hampered with intra-regional trade remaining exceptionally low compared to other regional blocs.
    - India can consider re-invigorating the Gujral doctrine with all the regional countries less Pakistan to encourage mutual cooperation for social and economic growth, recognizing the interconnectedness of the South Asian region.
  - ✓ **Focus on Afghan, Central Asian Republics (CAR) and Iran.**
    - Focus on Afghanistan, CAR and Iran by re-energizing Chabahar as well as bypassing Pakistan by promoting North South Transport Corridor.
    - The deep-rooted friendship and historical as well as cultural ties with Afghanistan need to be strengthened by extending a helping hand in the fields of education, medical and infrastructure development, as was done in the past. India has lost much in delaying its outreach to Taliban which has shown adequate promise and respect for historical ties between India and Afghanistan.

✓ **China.**

- Pakistan-China nexus is the most formidable and threatening challenge for India. It not only pose a two front threat to India but also complicates India's strategic approach to contain Pakistan. India would have to therefore adopt a multi-faceted approach leveraging diplomatic, economic, and strategic tools at its disposal.
- Exploring economic and military decoupling of Pakistan and China by exploiting Pakistan's stance on Uighurs.
- China's military exports to Pakistan not only embodies the spirit of defence cooperation but also provide an opportunity to China to validate its equipment in combat. India must repeatedly highlight the mediocrity of Chinese military equipment to denude the credibility of Chinese defence industry as demonstrated in Op SINDOOR post Pahalgam terrorist attack in 2025.
- Success of CPEC would further deepen Pakistan-China engagement. India must make every possible endeavor to undermine this project both by patronizing alternate connectivity initiatives and also standing in support with voices opposing exploitative character of CPEC especially in regions like GB, POJK and Baluchistan.
- Diplomatically, India can strengthen its partnerships with countries that have concerns about China's growing influence in the Indo-Pacific and beyond. This includes deepening ties with the United States, Japan, Australia (through the Quad), and European nations, as well as engaging with countries in Central Asia and the Middle East.
- By continuing to highlight Pakistan's issues with terrorism, political instability and financial mismanagement in global forums, India can make it more challenging for China to consistently portray Pakistan as a stable and reliable partner for its long-term strategic goals.

- **Bilateral.**
  - ✓ **Water as a Weapon.**
    - India has recently suspended the IWT with Pakistan after the Pahalgam terrorist attack. India has always displayed compliance with the IWT, often miscalculating its own generosity. But post the terrorist attack India has explicitly demonstrated that terror and water cannot go hand in hand.
    - As a responsible upper riparian state, India must optimise the entire provisions of the treaty by utilising the permissible storage capacity of 3.6 Million Acre Feet (MAF) on the Western rivers. Due to poor water development projects, 2 to 3 MAF of India's share easily flows into Pakistan. Similarly, out of the total estimated capacity for 11,406 MW of electricity, only 3034 MW has been tapped so far.[3]

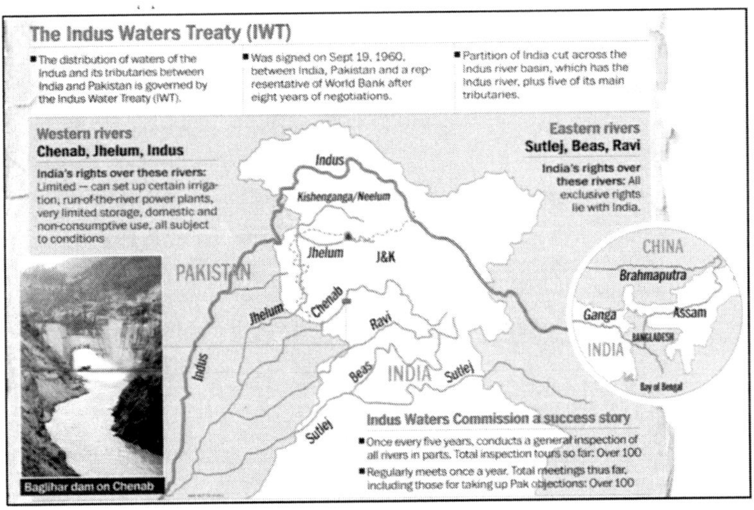

Figure 7.1: Indus Water Treaty

    - Kabul River is a major trans-boundary river across Afghanistan and Pakistan. The need for an agreement on water sharing of Kabul River which is a major tributary of Indus is becoming increasingly important for Pakistan due to its burgeoning population and allied water scarcity problems.[4] For Afghanistan, improving its power and water infrastructure is important for jumpstarting its economy. Kabul River impacts the internal security of Afghanistan and is much more than just being a tool of coercive diplomacy against Pakistan.[5] India must support Afghanistan's claims over water of Kabul River which is its legitimate right.

- As per studies on the subject, there is 75-95% probability of water wars in the next 50 to 100 years. Climate change has enhanced the competition for this critically scarce resource. Indus basin lies amongst one of the five most vulnerable water hotspots identified in the world.[6] It is therefore imperative for India to utilise its 100% share of Western rivers and also revive the pending project of constructing 12 dams on the Kabul River basin with Afghanistan. These projects on its either border would further starve the already water-stressed Pakistan.

✓ **Wolf Warrior Relationship.**

- "Yes, the Indian Foreign Service has changed. Yes, they follow the orders of the Government. Yes, they counter the arguments of others. No, it's not called arrogance. It is called confidence. And it is called defending National Interest", as stated by Dr S. Jaishankar while speaking in the Parliament on 21 May 2022 highlights the future contours of India's foreign policy[7]
- India today needs to adopt a Wolf Warrior diplomacy, so as to be assertive in global forums while being confrontational and combative, especially against Pakistan, in securing its national interests.
- India needs to consistently red flag Pakistan's excesses and highlight the atrocities and persecution of the people of Baluchistan, KPK and PoJK in UN and other global and international forums. At diplomatic and global front, we must not hesitate in bringing to fore the marginalisation of minorities to include Hindus, Sikhs, Christians and even certain Muslim sects within Pakistan.

- Economic forums must be exploited to highlight Pakistan and its Army's disruptive financial actions with an aim to rein it down with stringent austerity measures. Limiting conditions should be imposed on Pakistan for seeking additional loans to ultimately make its economy more fragile. Pakistan's financial irregularities, hawala transactions and connections with terror groups must be exposed to place it yet again in FATF Grey/ Black list.

✓ **IW Campaign.**

- Perception management and IW is the most effective vector available to give required traction to Pakistan's fault lines. Atrocities committed by Pakistan, human rights violations and mass disappearances must be highlighted through a well conceptualized and planned IW campaign. The regional affiliations and attuned demands for 'greater autonomy/ independent states' should be emphasized through scientific toolkits to bring out the suppression of civil liberties in restive regions of Pakistan. The vulnerabilities of CPEC can also be strategically exploited to put both Pakistan and China on the back foot.
- Pak Army must be discredited by highlighting its unfair meddling in Pakistan's politics, economy and foreign affairs. Similarly, dominance of Punjab in Pakistan's politics, bureaucracy, ubiquitous military and economy should also be discredited to further accentuate the fault lines in the society. The provinces of Baluchistan, KPK and Sindh have been ignored for long by successive Governments. These regions are worst affected due to shortage of food, water and other basic amenities. The dwindling human development index in these regions must be exposed at various regional and global forums.
- People of PoJK and GB have to be exposed to the Indian 'development oriented approach' vis-à-vis 'centre of terror ideology' adopted by Pakistan. Pakistan's lack of faith in the

local population of PoJK and the continued neglect of GB by the government needs to be exposed. Underdeveloped infrastructure, high taxes, exploitation of local resources and lack of employment for local youth in PoJK should be highlighted to draw comparison with J&K which has been bearing the fruits of progressive development in the recent years.

- The influencer world has far outreach and widespread coverage across all strata of the society. This potent tool has to be tapped innovatively to expose the shortcomings of the government and indiscriminate abuse of power by Pakistan Army. Social media has undeniably played a transformative role in spurring and shaping revolutions across the globe. This lever can fundamentally alter the dynamics of political mobilization in Pakistan and create conditions for a purple spring which would alter the course of Pakistan for several years to come.

  Own intelligence agencies must also invest in cultivating disenchanted and gullible Pakistan diaspora including service veterans who can play an important role in discrediting the Pakistani establishment.

- **Internal.**

  ✓ **Catalysing the Anarchy.**

  - The supremacy of elected civil government and respect for right balance of power remains elusive in Pakistan. In Pakistan national interests are sacrificed for short-term political gains. This weak character of democratic ideology in Pakistan has led to internal instability which should be exploited to the advantage of India. India must leverage the political fissures to expose Pakistan as a challenged democracy on the global arena while covertly fuelling this civil - military rift.

  - Judiciary has been a controversial participant in the public affairs of Pakistan. Its tainted verdicts since many decades have followed the 'Doctrine of Necessity' (making lawful by necessity, which is otherwise unlawful). This infirmity in the overall construct of governance needs to be exploited to demonstrate the fragility and vulnerability of Pakistan as a nation.

- Pakistan Army has a military economy of its own and follows the 'Culture of Entitlement'. India must bring to light the commercial stakes of Pakistan's Armed Forces which takes precedence over the national interest of Pakistan. Financial assistance and loan packages by IMF and other institutions should be based on the conditionality that no money should inflow into businesses controlled or owned by Pakistan Armed Forces.
- The anarchy or chaos in Pakistan will increase when the population of Pakistan would get disenchanted against its own military. India must leverage its proxies in Baluchistan, Sindh and KPK to shape the international opinion on the atrocities and human rights violations committed against the civilians, to include arrests without warrants, disappearances, mass killings, rape and murder of innocent women and girls in the restive provinces.

✓ **Keep the Ethno-Nationalism Faultline Alive.**

- India's aim must be to highlight the regional movements in Pakistan as 'Nationalist Struggle' at different international platforms showcasing their plight and cause. Creation of favourable narratives will be the key to success.
- India must reserve seats in the Parliament for PoJK and appoint expats as members of the Parliament. They would be an asset towards accentuating India's narrative of development, secularism and inclusiveness in J&K while highlighting the dilapidated condition of people living in PoJK on the contrary.
- Situation of a 'stifling democracy' in Pakistan will create greater mess and increase the possibility of its break up. For this purpose, it is necessary to widen the gap between the moderates and extremists and fuel ideological divides, majorly between the liberal Barelvis and more conservative Deobandis.

- India must look at enhancing the activities of proxies in creating public disorder. This would further accentuate the narrative of Pakistan being a failed state. Also, attempts should be made to keep the pot boiling along the Afghanistan-Pakistan border due to conflicting claims. Security of CPEC should remain a concern in Pakistan with potent threat from TTP, BLA and BLF besides other major nationalist groups in KPK, Baluchistan and Sindh.
- Just as the Indian Council of Cultural Relations (ICCR) provide fellowship to the students of SAARC and African countries like Nigeria and Kenya, similarly we should invite applications (with relaxation in the eligibility criteria) from the students belonging to the regions of Baluchistan, Sindh, PoJK and GB. This will increase people-to-people contact with India and further strengthen their aspirations for equal opportunities in Pakistan. A favourable position by the beneficiaries of this program on India's claims at an opportune time would help in further isolating Pakistan.

✓ **Trigger the Pakistan Spring.**

- The emergence of Imran Khan's Tehreek-e-Insaaf (PTI) party has been a silver lining in the political landscape of Pakistan. Although Imran Khan remains in prison, his popularity as a mass leader provides an opportunity to mobilize the cadres of PTI to create conditions akin to large scale civil protests which would undermine the government. These protests could also be exploited to discredit Pakistan Armed Forces and expose fissures in public governance.
- India must highlight Pakistan's discriminatory educational policy against the Muslim and Non-Muslim minorities. Anti-government protests against rampant corruption in the country, rising unemployment, poverty and regional discrimination can fuel civil unrest. These protests once initiated can transform into a vicious cycle consuming the state and leading to disorder and anarchy.

- Dwindling human development index, food scarcity and water crisis must be exploited to let the Pak Spring bloom which would subsequently spiral on its own.
- Finally, the necessity of keeping democracy functional and people first approach should be highlighted aggressively by India.

- **Military.**
  - ✓ To deter Pakistan Army which considers belligerence against India as core of its existence, it is important to first and foremost ensure asymmetric enhancement and augmentation of own military capability.
  - ✓ All three services need to collaborate in all domains in a synergized manner to adapt and dominate the changing paradigm of warfare. India's military strategy must cater for required deterrence against both northern and western adversary which would require consistent efforts and dedicated allotment of defence budget.
  - ✓ While maintaining balance on both fronts, absolute moral and physical ascendency needs to be achieved both along the LC as well as in hinterland. In our approach to discredit Pakistan's proxy war in J&K, we need to ensure peace through surgical operations and a focused IW campaign.
  - ✓ There is again a need to strengthen then mechanism of Unified HQs and adopting a synergized approach. It must not be overlooked that response to Proxy War has to be delivered both in kinetic as well as non-kinetic domains across the entire spectrum ranging from strategic to tactical (STRACTICAL) operations. Important lines of effort at each level are deliberated in succeeding paragraphs.

Lines of Effort : Stractical Operations

Strategic Level. '33 Strategies of War',[8] by Robert Green gives out the broad contours of approach which India needs to adopt at strategic, operational and tactical level within the military domain. India's strategic construct would entail the following:

- **Righteous Strategy.** The fight to discredit Pakistan has to be leveraged from a higher moral ground by portraying Pakistani Army as evil in his intent and design. This can be done by openly questioning Pakistan's motives and by making the support base as narrow as possible. This contest has to be fought by India from a morally high position.
- **Deterrence Strategy.** As has been demonstrated by Op SINDOOR, own stance has to be made more and more threatening. The reputation of being a 'little menacing' with a streak of unpredictability has to be kept alive at all times. This will keep Pakistan deterred while enable India to focus on building conventional capabilities.
- **Ordinary-Extra Ordinary Strategy.** While making Pakistan believe that India's approach would always remain predictable, India must plan differently to surprise and disbalance Pakistan. Technology infusion in Tactics, Techniques and Procedures (TTPs) can help Indian armed forces in achieving this unexpected approach.
- **Annihilation Strategy.** As per this strategy, the enemy has to be surrounded from all sides and weakened in all dimensions. Likewise, Pakistan has to be strangulated economically, isolated diplomatically, neutralized in IW and defeated militarily thus annihilating his will power completely.

Operational Level. At the operational level, India's approach needs to be multi-dimensional where it transcends into both physical as well as cognitive spaces. It also must flow out from the strategic approach and facilitate the execution at tactical level. The way forward is recommended to be based on the following strategies:

- **Blitzkrieg Strategy.** The resistance, which has been built by Pakistan over the years along the LC should be overwhelmed with speed and suddenness. The capability of India's armed forces has to be built to such an extent that there is absolute superiority at multiple points of application thereby taking the enemy by surprise and forcing him into submission.
- **Intelligence Strategy.** Pakistan's has a professional military with adequate combat experience. To defeat them in their game, it is

important to read their minds, identify their weaknesses and exploit their vulnerabilities. Pre-emption of the enemy's move by understanding how their minds work can give rich dividends. The target as per this strategy is the mind of the adversary.

- **Misperception Strategy**. This strategy resonates with the military practice of deception where enemy is fed misinformation about own intentions. This needs to be achieved by weaving a seamless blend of fact and fiction. Misconceptions and decoys can consume the adversary and enable India to dictate the progress.
- **Centre of Gravity Strategy**. This strategy focuses on hitting the enemy where it hurts him the most. The source of power in Pakistan is the military leadership and the stature (fear) of Pakistani Army in public consciousness. By denuding this artificial halo created around Pakistan military, India would be able to dislocate the Centre of Gravity which lends strength to Pakistan.

Tactical Level. The success of overall strategy depends on successful execution of operations at the tactical level which is the cutting edge of any conflict. The recommended way forward entails the following strategies in tactical domain:

- **Fait-Accompli Strategy**. All-out war is neither affordable nor desirable. The best solution is therefore to take small bites, swallow little chunks (of territories) and present the resultant state as fait accompli. This strategy is followed by China which has succeeded in nibbling large areas slowly in almost all directions through 'Salami Slicing'. Nuanced execution of tactical operations is an essential pre-requisite for which necessary capabilities need to be developed in consonance with changing paradigm of warfare.
- **Inner Front Strategy**. By infiltrating into terrorist organizations through smart intelligence operations and working from within, Pakistan's evil nexus can be defeated slowly but surely. A strong tree gets eaten by termite and falls flat helplessly. Similarly, the Pakistani hybrid threat needs to be neutralized from within.
- **Strategy of the Void**. By removing all targets for the enemy and by not presenting any vulnerabilities which he can exploit, India can not only frustrate Pakistani Army but also fill him with a sense of

helplessness and desperation. It is therefore imperative that Pakistan is denied all targets and no triggers are allowed to be created for the nexus to take advantage of.

- **Exit Strategy**. Knowing how and where to end the things that too when it is advantageous to us is the acme of a sound exit strategy. An inconclusive cessation of operations (like the Ceasefire Agreement of 1948 and Shimla Agreement of 1972) can have far reaching repercussions. It is therefore important to visualize the desired end state and plan regressively in any tactical scenario.

Conclusion

Pakistan was born as an insecure state with Islam and revisionism as its core ideology. The predominance of military and Islam combined as deep state has been one of the biggest fault lines of Pakistan. Hatred for India is an endemic character of Pakistan's DNA. This clubbed with its Kashmir obsession, intense internal strife with secessionist fervours raging across restive provinces and troubled Western borders with Afghanistan has only accentuated its insecurities. A dominating Punjab and imposing Army undermines the autonomy and development of other regions of Pakistan. Terrorism which has been long exploited as a state policy has boomeranged and is consuming Pakistan today from the inside.

Pakistan has seen numerous democratic transitions, military coups, economic shudders, political crises and natural disasters. Surprisingly it has survived all the tremors and jolts so far. Today, Pakistan yet again finds itself at the cross roads marred by political and economic uncertainty. Its deeply entrenched fault lines stand exposed amidst fractured society and more assertive Army. The internal and external influences which have kept the ailing state integrated are shrouded in uncertainty. While China is concerned about the CPEC, US has become inconsistent with its policy on Pakistan. Opportunists like Turkey and OIC countries cannot be trusted too far. The future scenarios that have been appreciated are an outcome of this tumultuous situation in Pakistan which has a direct bearing on India's security calculus. It is therefore imperative for India to remain proactive at the moment and act as a catalyst rather being a spectator, to mould Pakistan's future contours as per its interests.

At present, Pakistan is in a fragile state. We have witnessed that a weak

Pakistan and vulnerable Pakistan military has always resorted to deflection, externalizing its problems onto India which has been their most preferred approach in crisis. Amidst all this, the world has remained oblivious with nations pre-occupied with their own insecurities in a VUCA environment. At the end of the day, the threshold for a full blown conventional conflict between two nuclear states with a violent history is extremely low. The only recourse that India has under the given circumstances is to keep Pakistan deterred which can only be achieved if it remains turbulent in perpetuity with chaos within. This state of anarchy would eventually discredit the complete security architecture in Pakistan leading to systemic failure of the nation state. Deduction of a state that has lost central control is neither delusional nor dramatic but a factual truth. It has been proven in the past and would get proved again with Baluchistan asserting self-control very soon in the near future. It is this state of a dis-integrated or fragmented Pakistan which is the most desirable scenario in relative terms. India must therefore amalgamate all its instruments of national power and adopt a 'Whole of Nation Approach' towards achieving this fragmentation of Pakistan in short term and Balkanization in due course. Pakistan which was born with a flawed identity in 1947 must resign to its fate of a beleaguered Pakistan in 2047 caused by wounds that have been self-inflicted over several years out of misplaced belligerence and hatred for India. It is only then that India would achieve its rightful place in the global stage exactly as suggested by our former President, who had said:

> *"Unless India stands upto the world, no one will respect us. In this world fear has no place only strength respects strength".*[9]
>
> **—Dr APJ Abdul Kalam.**

Notes

1 Ashley J. Tellis, "Are India's Strategic Goals in Pakistan Achievable?", Carnegie Endowment for International Peace, March 2019.

2 Greene Robert, (2007), "The 33 Strategies for War", Penguin Books, 2007.

3 Uttam Kumar Sinha, "Indus Water Treaty at 60: why there is a need to give it a fresh look", The Indian Express, 20 Sep 2020.

4 Fawad Ali, "Decades on - Pakistan is still seeking a Kabul River Agreement", The Third Pole, 05 May 2022

5 Waleed Majidyar, "Pakistan's Looming Water Conflict", 15 Dec 2018.

6 Where the water wars of the future will be fought, Big Think, The Present - 18 Oct 2018.

7 Times of India, 21 May 2022.

8 Greene Robert, (2007), "The 33 Strategies for War", Penguin Books, 2007.

9 www.englishphilosophy.in / abdul-Kalam-quotes/

Index